MW01614958

The Only
Investment Guide
You'll Ever Need

ALSO BY ANDREW TOBIAS

The Funny Money Game

Fire and Ice

Getting by on $100,000 a Year
(And Other Sad Tales)

Money Angles

The Invisible Bankers

Auto Insurance Alert!

My Vast Fortune

The Only Investment Guide You'll Ever Need

EXPANDED AND UPDATED THROUGHOUT

Andrew Tobias

A Harvest Original

Harcourt Brace & Company

San Diego   New York   London

Copyright © 1998, 1996, 1989, 1987, 1983, 1978 by Andrew Tobias

All rights reserved. No part of this publication may be reproduced or
transmitted in any form or by any means, electronic or mechanical, including
photocopy, recording, or any information storage and retrieval system, without
permission in writing from the publisher.

Requests for permission to make copies of any part of the work should
be mailed to: Permissions Department, Harcourt Brace & Company,
6277 Sea Harbor Drive, Orlando, Florida 32887-6777.

Quotation by John Templeton on page 122 reprinted courtesy of *Mutual Funds*
magazine.

ISBN 0-7394-0308-7

Designed by Cloyce Wall

Printed in the United States of America

To my broker—even if he has,
from time to time, made me just that.

Contents

Preface

If it is brassy to title a book *The Only Investment Guide You'll Ever Need*, it's downright brazen to revise it. Yet not to do so would have been worse, partly because so much has changed, and partly because so many people, against all reason, have continued to buy it.

In the 20 years since this book first appeared, the world has spun into high gear. Back then, checking accounts paid no interest and trading volume on the New York Stock Exchange averaged 25 million shares a day. (Today, 400 million shares are described on the Nightly News as "slow trading.") Back then, about three people had ever heard of personal computers. The largest mutual fund family offered a choice of 15 different funds. Today: 240.

There were no cash management accounts, no home equity loans, no 401(k) retirement plans or Roth IRAs, no universal life-insurance policies, no index funds, WEBS or spiders, no program trading, no frequent-flier miles (*oh, no!*), no zero-coupon bonds, no leveraged buyouts, no master limited partnerships, no global shift toward free-market economics, no automatic teller networks, no CNBC, no Internet—not even a Home Shopping Network. (How did anyone ever *buy* anything?)

The top federal income tax bracket was 70%.

The basics of personal finance haven't changed—they never do. And there are still just a relatively few common-sense things you need to know about your money. But the welter of investment choices and the thicket of jargon and pitches have grown a great deal more dense. Perhaps this book can be your machete.

Acknowledgments

I would like to thank Sheldon Zalaznick and Clay Felker, the editors with whom I worked most closely at *New York* magazine when this book was first written . . . Less Antman, for persuading me to revise it—and for providing a tremendous amount of excellent help, insight and good humor in the bargain . . . Carol Hill, my editor on the original edition, and Michael Stearns, Christa Malone, and Beverly Fisher, my editors and boosters on this one . . . Ibbotson Associates for their market statistics . . . Jerry Rubin, Bart Barker and Paul Harrison, among many others from the computer software world . . . John and Rochelle Kraus, Laura Sloate, Martin Zweig, Burton Malkiel, Alan Abelson, Yale Hirsch, Charlie Biderman, Paul Marshall, Robert Glauber, Murph and Nancy Levin, Jesse Kornbluth, Jack Egan, Marie Brenner, Don Trivette, Peter Vanderwicken, Eugene Shirley, John Koten, Audrey Schneider, Jane Berentson and Charles Nolan . . . *Forbes,* the *Wall Street Journal* and the *New York Times*. Although much of what I know I have learned from these people and institutions, whatever egregious faults you—or they—may find with this book are strictly my own.

The Only
Investment Guide
You'll Ever Need

Minimal Risk

*There is no dignity quite so impressive, and no independence
quite so important, as living within your means.*

—CALVIN COOLIDGE

If I'm So Smart, How Come This Book Won't Make You Rich?

You have to watch out for the railroad analyst who can tell you the number of ties between New York and Chicago, but not when to sell Penn Central.

—NICHOLAS THORNDIKE

Here you are, having just purchased a fat little investment guide we'll call *Dollars and Sense,* as so many investment guides are (although the one I have in mind had a different title), and you are skimming through idea after idea, growing increasingly excited by all the exclamation marks, looking for an investment you would feel comfortable with. You page through antique cars, raw land, mutual funds, gold— and you come upon the section on savings banks. Mexican savings banks.

The book explains how by converting your dollars to pesos you can earn 12% on your savings in Mexico instead of 5½% here. At 12% after twenty years, $1,000 will grow not to a paltry $2,917, as it would at 5½%, but to nearly $10,000! What's more, the book explains, U.S. savings banks report interest payments to the Internal Revenue Service. Mexican banks guarantee not to. Wink.

The book does warn that if the peso were devalued relative to the dollar, your nest egg would shrink proportionately. But, the author reassures, the peso is one of the stablest currencies in the world, having been pegged at a fixed rate to the dollar for 21 years; and the Mexican government has repeatedly stated its intention not to devalue.

Now, how the heck are you, who needed to buy a book to tell you about this in the first place, supposed to evaluate the stability of the Mexican peso? You can only assume that the author would not have devoted two pages to the opportunity if he thought it were a poor risk to take—and *he's* an expert. (Anyone who writes a book, I'm pleased to report, is, ipso facto, an expert.) And, as a matter of fact, you do remember reading somewhere that Mexico has *oil*—pretty good collateral to back any nation's currency. Anyway, what would be so dreadful if, as your savings were doubling and tripling south of the border, the peso *were* devalued 5% or 10%?

So, scared of the stock market and impressed by the author's credentials, you take *el plunge*.

And for 18 months you are getting all the girls. Because while others are pointing lamely to the free clock radios they got with their new 5½% savings accounts, you are talking Mexican pesos at 12%.

Comes September, and Mexico announces that its peso is no longer fixed at the rate of 12.5 to the dollar, but will, instead, be allowed to "float." Overnight, it floats 25% lower, and in a matter of days it is down 40%. Whammo. Reports the *New York Times*: "Devaluation is expected to produce serious immediate difficulties, most conspicuously in heavy losses for Americans who have for years been investing dollars in high-interest peso notes." How much is involved? Oh, just $6 or $8 *billion*.

You are devastated. But you were not born yesterday. At least you will not be so foolish as to join the panic to withdraw your funds. You may have "bought at the top"—but you'll be damned if you'll sell at the bottom. The peso could recover somewhat. Even if it doesn't, what's lost is lost. There's no point taking your diminished capital out of an account that pays 12% so you can get 5½% in the United States.

And sure enough, in less than two weeks the float is ended, and the Mexican government informally repegs the peso to the dollar. (Only now one peso is worth a nickel, where two weeks ago it was worth eight cents.) You may not know much about international finance (who does?), but you know enough to sense that, like a major house-cleaning, this 40% devaluation in Mexico's currency ought to hold it for a long, long time. In fact, you tell friends, for your own peace of mind you're just as glad they did it all at once rather than nibbling you to death.

And then six weeks later the peso is floated again, and slips from a nickel to less than four cents. Since Labor Day, you're down 52%.

Aren't you glad you bought that book?

(Everything changes and nothing changes. That was 1976. In 1982 the peso was devalued again—by 80%. In the winter of 1994–95, it dropped 55%. Then ... well, you get the idea.)

This immodestly titled book—the title was the publisher's idea, in a weak moment I went along—is for people who have gotten burned getting rich quick before. It is the only investment guide you will ever need *not* because it will make you rich beyond any further need for money, which it won't, but because *most* investment guides you *don't* need.

The ones that hold out the promise of riches are frauds. The ones that deal with strategies in commodities or gold are too narrow. They tell you *how* you might play a particular game, but not whether to be playing the game at all. The ones that are encyclopedic, with a chapter on everything, leave you pretty much where you were to begin with—trying to choose from a myriad of competing alternatives.

I hasten to add that, while this may be the only investment guide you will ever need, it is by no means the only investment guide that's any good. But, sadly, reading three good investment guides instead of one will surely not triple, and probably not even improve, your investment results.

The odd thing about investing—the frustrating thing—is that it is not like cooking or playing chess or much of anything else. The more cookbooks you read and pot roasts you prepare, the better the cook—within limits—you are likely to become. The more chess books you read and gambits you learn, the more opponents—within limits—you are likely to outwit. But when it comes to investing, all these ordinarily admirable attributes—trying hard, learning a lot, becoming intrigued—may be of little help, or actually work against you. It has been amply demonstrated, as I will document further on, that a monkey with a handful of darts will do about as well at choosing stocks as most highly paid professional money managers. Show me a monkey that can make a decent veal parmesan.

If a monkey can invest as well as a professional, or nearly so, it stands to reason that you can, too. It further stands to reason that, unless you get a kick out of it, you needn't spend a great deal of time reading investment guides, especially long ones. Indeed, the chief virtue of this one (although I hope not) may be its brevity. This one is about the forest, not the trees. Because if you can find the right forest—the right overall investment outlook—you shouldn't have to worry much about the trees. Accordingly, this book will summarily dismiss investment fields that some people spend lifetimes wandering around in. For example: It is a fact that 90% or more of the people who play the commodities game get burned. I submit that you have now read all you need ever read about commodities.

This thing about the forest and the trees—about one's degree of perspective—bears further comment, particularly as for many of us it is second nature to feel guilty if we "take the easy way out" of a given situation. If, for example, we read the flyleaf and first and last chapters of a book, to get its thrust, instead of every plodding word.

I raise this not only because it could save you many hundreds of hours stewing over investments that will do just as well unstewed, but also because it leads into the story of The Greatest Moment of My Life.

The Greatest Moment of My Life occurred in the Decision Analysis class at Harvard Business School. Harvard

Business School uses "the case method" to impart its wisdom, which, on a practical level, means preparing three or four cases a night for the following day's classroom analysis. Typically, each case sets forth an enormous garbage dump of data, from which each student is supposed to determine how the hero or heroine of the case—inevitably, an embattled division manager or CEO—should ideally act. Typically, too, I could not bring myself to prepare the cases very thoroughly.

The format of the classroom discussion was that 75 of us would be seated in a semicircle with name cards in front of us, like United Nations delegates, and the professor would select without warning whomever he thought he could most thoroughly embarrass to take the first five or ten minutes, solo, to present his or her analysis of the case. Then everyone else could chime in for the rest of the hour.

On one such occasion, we had been asked to prepare a case the nub of which was: What price should XYZ Company set for its sprockets? Not coincidentally, we had also been presented with a textbook chapter containing some elaborate number-crunching way to determine such things. The theory behind it was simple enough—charge the price that will make you the most money—but the actual calculations, had one been of a mind to do them, were extremely time-consuming. (This was just before pocket calculators reached the market.)

The professor, a delightful but devious man, noting the conspicuous absence of paperwork by my station, had the out-and-out malevolence to call on me to lead off the discussion. I should note that this occurred early in the term, before much ice had been broken and while everyone was still taking life very seriously.

My instinct was to say, with contrition: "I'm sorry, sir, I'm not prepared"—a considerable indignity—but in a rare moment of inspiration I decided to concoct a bluff, however lame. (And here is where we get, at last, to the forest and the trees.) Said I: "Well, sir, this case obviously was meant to get us to work through the elaborate formula we were given to determine pricing, but I didn't do any of that. The case said that XYZ Company was in a very competitive industry, so I figured it couldn't charge any *more* for its sprockets than everyone else, if it wanted to sell any; and the case said that the company had all the business that it could handle—so I figured there would be no point in charging *less* than everyone else, either. So I figured they should just keep charging what everybody else was charging, and I didn't do any calculations."

Ahem.

The professor blew his stack—but not for the reason I had expected. It seems that the whole idea of this case was to have us go round and round for 55 minutes beating each other over the head with our calculations, and *then* have the professor show us why the calculations were, in this case, irrelevant. Instead, the class was dismissed 12 minutes after it began—to thunderous applause, I might add—there being nothing left to discuss.*

Now, let me return to commodities.

My broker has, from time to time, tried to interest me in commodities. He trades commodities for many of his clients and—almost as proof of his faith in the product—for his own account as well. He has direct access to the head commodities man at his firm, a major New York brokerage house. He tells of clients who have churned $5,000 into $500,000.

"John," I ask, "be honest. Do *you* make money in commodities?"

"Sometimes," he says.

"Of course, *sometimes*," I say, "but overall do you make money?"

"I'm making money now. I'm up $3,200 on May [pork] bellies."

---

* Herewith a list of all my other triumphs at Harvard Business School: I graduated.

"But overall, John, if you take all the money you've made, minus your losses, commissions, and taxes, and if you divide that by the number of hours you've spent working on it and worrying about it—what have you been earning an hour?"

My broker is no fool. "I'm not going to answer that," he sort of gurgles.

It turns out that my broker has made around $5,000 before taxes in four years of commodities trading. Without a $10,000 profit once in cotton and a $5,600 profit in soybeans he would have been massacred, he says—but of course that's the whole idea in this game: a lot of little losses but a few enormous gains. He can't *count* the number of hours he's spent working on and worrying about commodities. He went home short sugar one Friday afternoon after it had closed up-limit (meaning that he was betting it would go down, but instead it went up so fast he didn't have time to cover his bet, and now he stood to lose even more than he had wagered) and spent the entire weekend, and his wife's entire weekend, worrying about it. So maybe this very smart broker, with his very smart advisors, and their very smart computer readouts, has made $2 or $3 an hour, before taxes, for his effort. And he wants *me* to play? He wants *you* to play?

If 90% of the people who speculate in commodities lose (and 98% may be a more accurate figure), the question, clearly, is how to be among the 10% (or 2%) who win. If it is not just a matter of luck, then it stands to reason that the players who have the best chance are insiders at the huge firms—Hershey, Cargill, General Foods, etc.—who have people all over the world reporting to them on the slightest change in the weather, and who have a minute-to-minute feel for the market (whether it be the market for cocoa, wheat, or what-have-you). You are not such an insider, but those who are would be delighted to have you sit down at the table and play with them.

If, on the other hand, it *is* just luck, then you have just as good a chance as anybody else for the jackpot, and all you're doing is gambling, plain and simple, hoping to be lucky, and paying commission after commission to a broker who, friend or brother-in-law though he may be, cannot bring himself to give you the right advice. He'll give you advice on October broilers or the frost in Florida or the technician's report he claims somehow to have seen before anybody else. Gladly. What he won't tell you—or it will cost him dearly if he does—is that you shouldn't be in the game at all.

Class dismissed.

Similarly: antique cars, wines, autographs, stamps, coins, diamonds, art. For two reasons. First, in each case you are competing against experts. If you happen already to be an expert, then you don't need, and won't pay any attention to, my advice anyway. Second, what most people fail to point out as they talk of the marvelously steady appreciation of such investments is that, while what you would have to *pay* for a given lithograph might rise smartly every year (or might not), it's not so easy for the amateur to turn around and sell it. Galleries usually take half the retail price as their cut—so a print that cost $100 and appreciated in five years to $200, retail, might bring you all of $100 when you went back to the gallery to sell it. Meanwhile, neither print nor wine nor diamonds nor Rolls would have been paying you dividends (other than psychic); indeed, you would have been paying to insure them.

I gave a speech to this effect in Australia many years ago, just as the first faint flaws were beginning to appear in what was then a very hot diamond market. Nothing is forever, I suggested, not even the 15% annual appreciation of diamonds. When I finished, a mustachioed gentleman with a bushy head of previously owned hair came up to say how much he agreed with my remarks. "Diamonds!" he scoffed (you could see the disgust in his face). And for a minute there I thought I had met a kindred spirit. *"Opals!"* he said. *"That's* where the money is!" The fellow, it developed, was an opal salesman.

As a child, I collected "first-day covers" (colorful, specially postmarked envelopes to commemorate the issuance of a new stamp). Sure enough, every year they cost me more and more. Decades later, discovering them in the back of a closet, I called a local collector I had reason to know was on the acquisition trail. (I saw his notice on the supermarket bulletin board.) Knowing you always do better if you can cut out the middleman, I figured on selling them to him direct. These are beautiful first-day covers we are talking about, from the forties and fifties—hundreds of them. They had cost anywhere from 25 cents on up (although, in those days, so had a week in the country).

"How much does your collection weigh?" the buff asked, once I had suitably whetted his interest.

"How much does it *weigh?*" I asked. "Is your collection on a diet? It weighs a few pounds, I guess."

"I'll give you $25 for it," he said. Checking around, I found this was not an unfair price. I'm going to wait another twenty years and try again.

Commemorative medallions (and so forth) issued ad nauseam as "instant collectors' items" by the Franklin Mint served to make the original shareholders of the Franklin Mint rich but are much less likely to do the same for you. Their silver, gold or platinum content is only a fraction of the selling price.

Gold itself pays no interest and costs money to insure. It is a hedge against inflation, all right, and a handy way to buy passage to Liechtenstein, or wherever it is we're all supposed to flee to when the much ballyhooed collapse finally materializes. But if you're looking for an inflation hedge, you might do better with stocks or real estate. In the long run, they will rise with inflation, too. And in the short run, they pay dividends and rent.*

---

* As of this revision, dividends have largely gone out of style. It's a tax thing. (And a euphoria thing.) But they'll be back.

Broadway shows are fun to invest in, but even if the show you back gets rave reviews, you are likely to lose. A show can linger on Broadway for a year or more, with packed houses on the weekends, and not return its backers a dime.

Chain letters never work.

Things that look like cosmetics companies but are really chain letters in disguise, where the big money to be made is not in selling cosmetics but in selling franchises to sell franchises (to sell cosmetics), don't work either.

Things that involve a personal salesman who is full of enthusiasm at the prospect of making you rich don't work. The richer he hopes to make you, the faster you should run.

There are, in fact, very few ways to get rich quick. Fewer still that are legal. Here's one: Take $5,000 (borrow it if you have to), place it on 22 at the nearest roulette table, and win $175,000. Don't laugh. Many complicated schemes, if they were stripped of their trappings and somehow reduced to their underlying odds, would be not much less risky. It's the trappings—the story, the pitch—that obscure the odds and persuade people to ante up the $5,000 they'd never dream of betting at roulette.

Anyway, enough of the things that won't do you much good and on to some things that might. The goal of the next chapter is to save you $1,000 a year. Maybe more.

A Penny Saved Is Two Pennies Earned

"I walked home to save bus fare."

"Gee, you could have saved a lot more by not taking a taxi."

—OLD JOKE

You are in a higher tax bracket than you think. At least, most people are. And this number—your tax bracket—is critical to understanding your finances.

If you earn $30,000 and pay $3,000 in federal income tax, that does *not* mean you are in the 10% tax bracket (any more than if you earn $230,000 and pay $23,000). On *average,* you are paying 10% of your income in federal tax, but that's not what's important. What's important in making financial decisions is how much tax you pay on the margin—on the last few dollars that you earn.

Because the income tax is graduated, you pay no tax on the first few dollars you earn but a lot on the last few. That may average out to 10%; but, in the case above, if you earned another $1,000 and you're single, nearly 36% of it would go straight to the government ($280 in federal income tax, another $76.50 in Social Security tax), and *that's* your tax bracket: 36%. Unless you happen to be self-employed (add another 7.65%) and/or subject to local income taxes as well (add some more). In New York City—admittedly, the most brutal example possible—it's not hard to find subway riders, never mind guys in limos, in close to the 50% tax bracket.

To figure your own tax bracket, should you be of a mind to, just haul out last year's federal and local tax returns and calculate how much more tax you would have had to pay if you had earned an extra $1,000.* If you'd have had to fork over $350 of this hypothetical $1,000 bonus in taxes, you're in the 35% tax bracket.

Add in sales tax and property taxes, of course, and the bite is even worse. But such taxes, which are not directly tied to what you earn, don't count in figuring your tax bracket. (Neither does Social Security tax when making many decisions, since it is not levied on investment income and is not reduced by charitable or other "deductions.")

For the sake of simplicity, even though it's a bit of an exaggeration for most people, let us assume you are in the 50% bracket, or not far from it. Do you know what that means?

It means that if your boss gave you a $1,000 bonus or raise, you would get to keep $500.

It means that "time-and-a-half for overtime," since it's all earned on the margin, is not such a posh deal after all. After taxes, it may be no more valuable to you than any other "time."

It means, above all, that a penny saved—not spent—is *two* pennies earned.

Consider: If you were planning to go out for dinner tomorrow night, as you do every Thursday night, for around $50 with the tip . . . but you ate at home instead for $10 . . . you'd have saved $40. To *earn* an extra $40, you'd actually have had to earn $80: half for you, half for the tax men.

My point is not that we pay too much in taxes. For whatever comfort it may provide (not much), we get off pretty easy relative to the citizens of most other nations—though we could certainly do a smarter job of deciding

----

* If you use a computer to do your taxes, this calculation is easy. Otherwise, you can get a general idea just by looking at the printed tax tables in the tax booklet the IRS sends you each year—or check www.irs.ustreas.gov. (Note that any additional local taxes would be partially offset by a federal tax deduction—if you itemize your deductions.)

what to tax and how to spend the proceeds. My point, rather, is that when Ben Franklin said "A penny saved is a penny earned," there *was* no income tax. There *was* no Social Security Tax. The updated adage would read: "A penny saved is *two* pennies earned." Or nearly so.

So if you want to pile up a little nest egg, or a big one, the first thing you might consider—even though you've doubtless considered it before—is spending less rather than earning more. Which is what this chapter's about. If you're in the 50% tax bracket, it's twice as effective—and often easier.

Charles Revson, the late cosmetics tycoon, bought his mouthwash by the case. By doing so, although it was the furthest thing from his mind, he did better investment-wise than he ever did in the stock market. In the stock market, with his Revlon-made fortune, Revson perennially blew tens of thousands of dollars on one or another specula-tion. But on Cepacol he was making 20% or 30% a year, tax-free.

He made it two ways: the discount he got for buying the super-economy size, in bulk; and the discount he got, in effect, by beating inflation. He got a year's worth, or two, at last year's price. If he had kept the money he spent on Cepacol in a savings account at 5%—for him, 2% after tax—and taken it out bit by bit to buy Cepacol in the one-at-a-time $1.19 size, where would he have been?

The lesson is clear, even if you are one of those people with naturally pleasant breath.

Say you're a couple who drink one bottle of red wine every Saturday night. And say, to keep the math simple, you go for the fancy stuff—$10 a bottle. Say, finally, your wine shop is like mine: it offers a 10% discount if you buy by the case. What kind of "investment return" can you "earn" buying by the case? Ten percent? No, it's better than that.

The old way, you paid out $10 every week. Buying by the case, you lay out $108 ($120 for twelve bottles, minus the 10% discount). That means tying up an extra $98, but "earning" a $1 discount on every bottle for doing so. In the course of the year, that comes to $52. Gosh! That's quite a reward for keeping, at most, an extra $98 tied up throughout the year. It works out to better than a 53% return—tax-free, no less, since the IRS doesn't tax you for smart shopping.*

The point is not to save $12 on a case of wine, but to do as much of your buying this way as is practical. In the aggregate, it might tie up an extra $1,000. But between beating inflation by buying now and buying in bulk when items are on sale (or getting a by-the-case discount), you could easily stretch $1,000 to buy $1,400 of the very same stuff you'd have bought in the course of the year anyway. And that's a 40% tax-free return on your money—$400 you've managed to save in the course of the year—*with no sacrifice whatever.* It's not enough to make you rich, but neither is $1,000 in a savings bank.

This is the chickenhearted way to play commodities, guaranteed safe for all but compulsive eaters. Forget pork bellies on 10% margin and all those other near-surefire ways to get fried. I am "long," as of this writing, a case of Snackwell low-fat vanilla cream cookies, a case of private-label tissue paper, a virtual lifetime supply of trash-can liners, several kegs of Heinz ketchup, and much more. I was "short" sugar years ago, when it ran up to the moon, which is to say I wouldn't buy any. I just ate down my inventory. Wholesale sugar prices subsequently fell from 64 cents back down to 9 cents and I went "long" a few pounds.

Where to put this mountainous investment? Besides the obvious, like a pantry or basement, if you have such spacious digs, you might also consider stashing your hoard under a bed or table, with a bedspread or tablecloth over the top. I know this is absurd, but I'll bet you can fit thirty cases of staples under just one table. Or make it a bench

---

* Well, actually it works out to 177%—see the appendix for details.

and put a board over it, with a cushion. Water jugs, bouillon cubes, a can opener (don't forget that!)—plan your portfolio, which doubles as a disaster hoard, and buy it on sale, in bulk. (If you're hoarding tuna, you've obviously got to hoard mayonnaise, too.)

This idea of a disaster hoard, by the way, is not such a foolish one. Nor is it "gloom and doom." Disasters do occur . . . floods, earthquakes, power outages, . . . and it does make sense for every household to accumulate—now, when there's no need to, at sale prices—enough nonperishables to last a while. Such a modest stockpiling not only protects individuals, it serves the social interest as well. Just as the nation is stronger if there are strategic stockpiles, so is the social fabric a little less susceptible to disruption or panic if everyone has an added layer of security. Odd words in tranquil times—but harmless ones, at worst.

Don't tell me about botulism, either—out of 1.43 trillion cans of food sold between 1926 and 1994, only eight produced fatal cases of botulism. Canned food lasts for years (though soda does tend to go flat). And if you rotate your cases of food and drink, the way you used to rotate the sheets on your bed in camp—top to bottom, bottom to laundry, fresh one on top—you'll never let anything get too far out of date.

If this sort of investment takes up space, it also takes less effort: fewer trips to the store. And you are less likely to run out of things. I don't think there was a day in Charles Revson's life that his breath did not smell medicine-fresh.

What amazes me is that when I first wrote this, in 1978, almost no one did it. Sure, there were thrifty shoppers, and lots of people clipping coupons to get 25 cents off. But there were no Sam's Clubs or Price Clubs or Costcos. By 1995, according to *Fortune,* half of all U.S. households had shopped at a warehouse club.

If you haven't already, and there's one near you, *join it.* Don't be put off by the "membership requirements"—in the case of Costco, you have to pay $30 and be employed by certain kinds of organizations or be a business. If you don't qualify, just find someone who does—your local real estate agent, for example—to get you an "associate" card for $15.

Now here are a few more ways to save money:

• **Fly now, pay now.** *The simplest, safest, most sensible way to earn 18% or 20% on your money is to pay off your credit cards. Not having to pay 18% or 20% is as good as earning 18% or 20%.* Tax-free! Risk-free! It's folly to pay credit card interest if you can possibly avoid it.

Still, more than 60% of credit-card holders fail to pay them off within the grace period. In fact, many people keep money in a savings account, earning 2% or 3% after tax, at the same time as they are paying 20% to buy on time. They're earning 3 cents on each dollar with their left hand while paying out 20 cents with their right. That's a loss of 17 cents on every dollar—or, if theirs is a family perpetually $4,000 in hock, $680 a year, year after year. Wasted.

Credit cards are great for convenience, but terrible for borrowing. Either cut them up, if you can't pay on time; or—if you *can* pay on time—**make your credit cards pay you.** Use cards that give you cash back at the end of the year or frequent-flier miles or some other goody.

The Discover card (800-347-2683) rebates an average of ½% on the first $3,000 you charge each year, then 1%, and then—if you have their "private issue" card—2% above $5,000.

Frequent-flier cards give you a "mile" for each dollar you charge. Call 800-FLY-4444 for American, 800-537-7783 for United. If you have an American Express card (800-THE-CARD), sign up for their Express Miles program, where the miles you earn accumulate in a "bank" for transfer to your frequent-flier accounts at Delta, Continental, and USAir, among others. The Diners Club card (800-234-6377) gives you miles good on *all* U.S. airlines— and some other neat perks, as well.

The typical domestic "plan-ahead" ticket requires 25,000 miles, yet often saves me anywhere from $500 to

$1,250—2 to 5 cents a mile! That means I'm getting a "discount" of 2% to 5% on everything I charge. Not bad! (You should have seen me fighting with the sales manager when I bought my last car. He required a deposit and said I could put it on a credit card. So I naturally tried to put the *whole thing* on the card. An upside-down negotiation ensued, with me trying to give him the biggest possible deposit and him trying to take the smallest.) The nice thing about plan-ahead awards is that you don't necessarily have to plan ahead to get them. You do if you're trying to get a flight home for Thanksgiving. But if you run a small business and have to fly to Minneapolis for a day, there may well be seats available even a day before. It's in situations like that, where an economy ticket would otherwise have cost a fortune, that the value of the miles is particularly high.

Or get a nickel back on every dollar you charge, applied to the cost of your next new car (if you *buy* new cars)—call GM at 800-947-1000 or Ford at 800-285-3000 for details. Ask about their gold cards, too.

Most people go through life paying 18% extra for everything they charge because they don't pay their cards off on time . . . and getting nothing back because they use the wrong cards. Be one of the smart ones who *earn* 2% to 5%, tax-free, instead.

• **Fly now, pay less.** Especially if you find yourself wanting or needing to take a trip on short notice, when the best supersaver fares are gone—or without a Saturday night stay-over, without which there *are* no supersavers—try calling 800-PRICELINE or, if your child has a computer, get her to show you how to visit www.priceline.com. You just might save $300 at the cost of having to lay over for an hour in Chicago, say, is worth it to you, it's definitely worth a try.

• **Don't finance your car.** As with credit cards, not paying 11% on a car loan is as good as earning 11%. Risk-free! Tax-free!

"Ah," you are thinking. "Surely he is not now going to tell me I should pay off my mortgage." And I am not—although if it was taken out at 11%, and 7% mortgages are available as you read this, why, then, surely it has crossed your mind to refinance. And even paying down a 7% mortgage is not a *bad* investment. It's simply the equivalent of a completely safe 7% return. The difference between a house and a car is that a car depreciates, while a house, with any luck, appreciates. It may not be the sure thing it once was; and there are situations when it plainly makes more sense to rent. But there is a big difference between borrowing tax-deductibly to buy something that may appreciate and borrowing non-deductibly to buy something you merely consume.

Can't afford to buy a car for cash? Well, then . . .

• **Buy a used car.** That "new-car smell" is the most expensive fragrance in the world. It could be really depressing to *have to* do this. But when it's your own decision, to reach your own goals, that's another story. And it could save you many thousands of dollars.

• **Buy an economical car.** If you purchase a car that averages 30 miles to the gallon instead of 15 . . . and if an average gallon of gas over the next few years costs a buck twenty . . . then after having driven 25,000 miles you'll have saved $1,000, cash, on gas alone. What's more, the cars that get the best gas mileage often cost the least. This despite the fact that in terms of their most important feature by far—getting you where you're going—they are identical to the higher-priced models. By buying an "economy car" you save substantially on the purchase price, substantially on your insurance bill (the less expensive the car, the lower the theft and collision premiums), substantially on gas, substantially on maintenance, and substantially on interest (if you finance the purchase). In all, the financial decision to be "automotively frugal"—while it is a decision you have every right not to make—could mean as much to you as a $5,000 raise.

• **Resist the temptation to lease.** This is growing ever more popular but no more sensible. First off, it generally means a new car, so you're paying for that smell. Second, it means financing almost the entire thing—but with a hidden interest rate. (Hint: they're not hiding it because it's low.) Third, it's just a lot more complicated, with more potential pitfalls, than buying a car outright. If you're a budding salesperson, light on cash, who needs a new car to impress clients and who can deduct the cost for tax purposes, leasing may make sense. But if you're just driving to work or school or the supermarket, leasing is ordinarily the most expensive way to go.

• **Finance your car (if you must) with a home-equity loan.** One way to pay off your credit-card debt and your car loan is to borrow against the equity in your home, if you own one. Home equity loans are like huge credit cards you can draw on and pay back, in full or in part, as often as you like. They generally carry much lower interest rates than credit cards and somewhat lower rates than car loans; and the interest you pay is generally tax deductible. If you currently pay $3,000 a year in credit-card and car-loan interest, replacing all that debt with a home equity loan could save you $1,500 or more, between the lower interest rate and the value of the tax deduction.

The risk: you'll hock your home and then, credit junkie that you are, run those credit cards right back up again. If this sounds like you, take out the home equity loan but cut up all your credit cards.

And even then there are risks. What sense is there in taking out a 20-year loan to pay for a 6-year automobile? (Or a two-week vacation?) With nothing forcing you to pay off the loan over the life of the car, it's quite possible you won't. When it comes time to buy a new one, you'll just go deeper into debt. Instead of owning your home free and clear at retirement, you could find yourself mortgaged to the hilt. Wise use of a home-equity loan requires self-discipline.

If you do opt for a home-equity loan, as I have, seek a lender offering "no points" and minimal up-front fees.* That saves a chunk of cash, and you'll have lost less if you ever decide to move or refinance.

• **Don't be fooled by 1.9% financing.** When you see one of those deals offering 1.9% financing—or $1,500 cash back—*take the cash.* Otherwise, you're buying a $16,500 car for $18,000, albeit at a good low rate of interest. It's just one more way to lull you into paying more than you should.

(If you do have to finance the car, and if a home-equity loan doesn't work for you, your best bet will be a credit-union loan. If you don't belong to a credit union, your regular bank will often have a better rate than the dealership. Either way, promise me you'll buy the car based on its *total price,* not by comparing monthly payments. You'd be amazed how many people unwittingly pay $1,000 more than they need to for the car—and perhaps another extra $1,000 in interest—because the 60-month car loan made the payments lower than the 36-month loan. You want to borrow as little as possible, as cheaply as possible, for as short a time as possible.)

• **Haggle**—at least when it comes to buying or leasing cars. Since that can be distasteful and time consuming, consider 800-CAR-CLUB. You may well save time *and* money letting them do most of the work. (I haggled a little for you, too: refer to this book when you call, and they'll knock $20 off their fee.) A similar service is CarBargains—800-475-7283 (**or www.checkbook.org**). For $165, they get you five competitive bids from dealers near you; you then pick the lowest/nearest one. Both services have gotten lots of enthusiastic praise.

---

* Each point is 1% of the loan. Three points on a $100,000 loan equals $3,000, cash, up front. And on refinancings, points are *not* deductible all at once, but rather over the life of the loan—just $100 a year in the case of a 30-year loan with $3,000 in points.

• **Skip the trade-in.** Sure it's easier just to leave the old car there and drive off in the newly purchased one. Dealers know that and use it to their advantage. I would, too, if I were a dealer. But if you separate the buying and the selling, you are likely to come out ahead. Your goal: Get the best deal you can on the car you buy. Then get a decent deal on the car you sell, perhaps to a neighbor or through the classifieds or the Internet (see below).

• **Drive smoothly.** Rapid accelerations are murder on gas mileage; unnecessary braking converts energy, through friction, to heat. "Good driving habits," properly inflated tires, and a well-tuned engine can save as much as a third of a family's gasoline bill.

• **When buying auto or homeowner's insurance, shop around**—call GEICO (800-841-3000), among others, for a quote over the phone*—and "self-insure" by choosing the highest "deductible" you can comfortably afford. This usually means eating the first $500 or $1,000 of loss yourself, instead of $100 or $250. But unless you're dreadfully unlucky, your savings in premiums over a lifetime will more than cover the extra unreimbursed losses. This is especially true because even people who are fully insured hesitate to hit their insurance companies for small claims, knowing that their rates may go up if they do. Why pay for coverage you may not even use? Generally, there's no point in paying someone else to take a risk that you can afford to take yourself. After all, they're not doing it as a favor. They plan to make a profit even after paying all their overhead, marketing and sales costs. Why not keep all that yourself? Besides money, you'll save yourself the hassle and aggravation of making claims.

---

* Progressive Insurance offers not just its own quote over the phone (800-288-6776), but, in many states, rates for State Farm and two others as well—even when the competition offers a lower rate. So one call does the work of four. (In states where Progressive continues to specialize only in drivers with bad driving records, you'll get just their own quote.)

The ultimate deductible, of course, if you've bought a ratty old used car—my favorite kind—is to skip collision and theft coverage altogether. Who would steal it?

• **When buying life insurance, it's the same advice:** *shop around.* There are two basic kinds: "term" and "whole life" (also called "straight" or "ordinary" or "permanent" or "universal" or "variable"). With term insurance all you pay for—and get—is protection. If you die, they pay. With whole life you are buying a tax-sheltered savings plan as well. Your policy accumulates "cash values."

Term insurance rates start very low but go up every year. Whole-life rates start high but remain constant.

Insurance salesmen are eager to sell whole-life policies because their commissions are so much higher. But you would be wiser to buy renewable term insurance and do your saving separately. (With a renewable policy you are assured of continuing coverage even if your health deteriorates.)

The problems with whole life:

❖ Many policies pay low interest.

❖ It is impossible for a nonexpert to tell a good policy from a bad one.

❖ There is a tremendous penalty for dropping the policy, as many people do, after just a few years.

❖ Most young families can't afford the protection they need if they buy whole life. The same dollars will buy five or six times as much term insurance.

In later years, and particularly beyond the age of 50 or 55, term insurance premiums rise rapidly. But by then you may have a less urgent need for life insurance. The kids may be grown, the mortgage paid off, the pension benefits vested. You will still need to build substantial assets for retirement, and to protect your spouse; but there are better ways to save for old age than whole life.

To find a good low rate on term life insurance, call the

Wholesale Insurance Network (WIN) at 800-808-5810 and give them the information they need to send you a free packet of price quotes and applications. WIN gets a commission if you wind up buying—which you may, because there's a good chance they'll find you rates that beat what you're paying now. Two other free quote services to call: Insurance Quote Services at 800-972-1104 and Select Quote at 800-350-0100. Between the three of them, you should have more than enough good alternatives.

Also, if you live or work in Massachusetts, New York, or Connecticut, look into Savings Bank Life Insurance.

To determine how much life insurance you need—if any—see the appendix "How Much Life Insurance Do You Need?"

If you already have a whole-life policy, don't feel bad—and don't necessarily drop the policy. With hindsight, you might have done somewhat better buying term insurance and, say, putting the difference into an IRA. But you are building a valuable tax-advantaged nest egg, nonetheless. What's more, you've already paid the up-front charges; dropping the policy won't get them back. For an expert, personal evaluation of an investment-type policy you currently own or are considering, send $40 to James Hunt of the Consumer Federation of America Insurance Group (8 Tahanto St., Concord, NH 03301) along with the computer "illustration" that was used to sell you the policy. (If you can't find it, your agent or the insurance company can supply a new one. It shows, year by year, what you pay in and how the cash value grows.)

Insurance agents hate the phrase "buy term and invest the difference." They counter it by arguing people *won't* invest the difference—they'll squander it. And that is definitely a risk. But who's to say, if you're a squanderer, you're not also one of the great number of policyholders—something like 25%—who will let their expensive whole-life policies lapse within the first few years? That's *really* squandering it.

• **Skip insurance you *don't* need,** including: life insurance for children (a good buy only if your child is a movie star and you depend on his or her earning power); credit life insurance, offered as an option when you take out a loan (a good buy only for the elderly or terminally ill); flight insurance (a good buy never—only about a nickel of each dollar it costs goes to pay claims, the rest is marketing expense and profit); cancer insurance (it makes no sense to buy health insurance one disease at a time); car rental insurance (if your credit card or your own auto insurance policy covers you, as many do).

Skip particularly "appliance insurance"—extended warranties on your refrigerator or VCR or washer/dryer. Even if you remember you have this insurance years from now, when the appliance breaks, and even if the time you have to spend collecting on it is minimal—two big ifs—why pay someone to insure a risk you can afford yourself? Over the years, you will come out way ahead by resisting the salesman's attempts to sign you up.

• **Use the Internet.** In the first version of this book I suggested everyone get a copy of the Sears catalog, not necessarily to shop from it, but as a handy reference point for what everything cost. Ah, brave new world: that huge catalog has gone the way of manual typewriters. Now, as many of you know, there's something a thousand times more powerful—the Internet. If you're not already hooked in, a sense of what you can do might persuade you:

Want to send someone a book as a gift? Go to **www.amazon.com** or **www.barnesandnoble.com.** You save 30% and a great deal of time. Or try **www.bookblvd.com** to find the lowest price.

In the market for a car? Visit **www.edmunds.com** to find out what you should pay—or the value of the vehicle in your driveway. And check out **www.carclub.com** (which has humans who will actually negotiate a good price for you), **www.checkbook.org** (which sets neighborhood dealers bidding against each other for your business, and

www.auto-by-tel.com (which alerts local dealers to your interest).

Indeed, whether you're in the market to buy or sell a car *or just about anything else,* visit **www.classifieds2000.com.** Awesome. A moment ago, I asked for an air-conditioned Chrysler convertible with under 40,000 miles someplace in Florida. Bang—seconds later, I had nine Sebrings and Le-Barons to choose from and could send potential sellers an inquiry with the click of my mouse. So much for the old-fashioned newspaper classifieds. With **www.classifieds 2000.com** you can view or post ads for jobs, roommates, computers, baby strollers, sports memorabilia—you name it! Check it out. (Naturally, all the normal caveats apply to private transactions, just as they do with newspaper classifieds.)

Shopping for a good buy on life insurance or a good low rate to refinance your mortgage? Visit, among others, **www.quicken.com.** You could save more than enough to pay for your computer.

Want an appraisal on your home or some additional refinancing options? Check out **www.homeshark.com.**

Then there are **www.insureme.com,** a quote service to find the least expensive health, automobile, home-owners, and life insurance polices; **www.quotesmith.com,** another good service for health and life insurance; and **www.insure.com,** which teaches the ABCs of insurance and annuities . . . **www.el.com/elinks/taxes,** with links to many of the best sites on taxes; **www.irs.gov/forms_pubs/,** the place to get tax forms and instructions, and **www.irs.gov/ tax_edu/faq/** a useful IRS Taxpayer Help and Educa-tion site . . . **www.hsh.com** and **www.bankrate.com** and **www.banx.com** for locating good home and auto loan rates; **www.microsurf.com** for quotes on moving expenses and help selecting local realtors . . . **www.housenet.com,** about home maintenance, repairs, and improvements, and ways of reducing costs other than the mortgage . . . **www.travelocity.com** and **www.travelweb.com,** for airline prices, car rentals, and hotels . . . **www.teleworth.com** to help choose among long distance companies and plans based on your personal calling habits . . . **www.nolo.com** and **www.legaldocs.com** to consult before spending money on a lawyer.

The web is the whole world, and constantly changing/improving, so I won't even begin to try to catalog it all here. The main thing is: use it. It can save you money by cutting out the middleman (not that I don't feel sorry for him—I do), and by making it easy to compare prices.

• If you use a discount broker to buy and sell stocks, **use a *deep*-discount broker** (see page 156). You'll save even more.

• **Double-check your bank.** I have an adjustable-rate mortgage on an apartment building. OK, a very small apartment building in a very modest part of town. OK, a slum. The point is, it started out in February 1992 as a $400,000 mortgage at 7.5%, to be paid off ("amortized") over 10 years. After 12 months, I got a notice lowering my rate to 7% and telling me to pay $4,670.51 instead of the $4,748.07 I had been paying. In entering this into my computer,* I noticed they were asking for $17.22 a month more than they should. But on such a large loan, I figured I'd just chalk it up to not wanting to start "a thing."

After 12 more months, I got a notice that the interest rate would now be 7%—i.e., unchanged—yet telling me to pay a *different* monthly amount. Hello? I took a closer look and found that they showed my unpaid principal—the amount I still owed—as being about $7,000 higher than *Managing Your Money* thought it should be. Now this was getting serious. Seventeen bucks is one thing. Seven thousand is another. But the point I want to make here is: with-

---

* I use a program called *Managing Your Money*, which pays my bills by phone using a service called CheckFree. It used to pay my bills another way, too: I got a royalty from having helped create it. But that's over—the retail version of *Managing Your Money* is history—so consider *Quicken* for this kind of thing instead.

out checking, whether with my computer program or some other, who would have known? Who possibly has the kind of instincts that would tell him the unpaid principal on a loan like this should be $341,091.50 by April 1994, not $348,940.01? Dustin Hoffman in *Rainman*? Forget it! The man counted matches.

Brought to the bank's attention, it developed that they had hit me up for $6,800 plus interest in "force-placed insurance." The way that works: their computer looks for confirmation that your insurance has been renewed. If no one tells it "yes," then it sends you a notice telling you that the bank, to protect its interest, has "force-placed" a policy on the property at your expense, and, incidentally, this is the most expensive insurance policy in the history of the world. So you call and tell them, politely, to get their greedy little hands off your property—you did renew the insurance—and you fax them the renewal to prove it. They politely assure you that they won't hit you up for the insurance, after all. But, in this case, they did anyway. When I complained, I got a nice letter from the bank adjusting my unpaid balance down by $7,098.85.

Banks make mistakes. (Years ago, along with my bank statement, I once got the checks of a Chinese laundry. "What do you want me to do?" I asked the bank. "Send them to the laundry," answered the bank.) Especially with adjustable-rate mortgages, errors sometimes do creep in. Be sure to double-check your bank each time the payment is adjusted.

Note: Banks sometimes force-place insurance on car loans, too. Beware.

• **For help with college tuition,** call the Federal Student Financial Aid Information Center at 800-433-3243 and request their free information on government loans and grants.

• **Save energy.** Simple insulation (and even simpler weather-stripping) may be the best "investment" you can make, returning as much as 35% or more, tax-free, in annual savings on heating and cooling. Why put $1,000 into the stock of some utility and earn $60 in annual taxable dividends if you can put the same money into insulation and save $350—tax-free—on your utility bill? Check, also, the various credits that may be available to encourage such energy-saving investment. Your electric company will know about these, and may offer a free "energy audit" to show you how to cut your bills most effectively.

An excellent guide to cutting your energy bill is *Home-made Money,* by Richard Heede and the staff of the Rocky Mountain Institute ($14.95 from Brick House Publishing, 800-446-8642). You will learn that a single compact fluorescent lightbulb, in addition to saving you money and hassle, "can save enough coal-fired electricity over its lifetime to keep a power plant from emitting three-quarters of a ton of carbon dioxide (which contributes to global warming)" and that "full frostbelt use of today's best windows would more than displace Alaska's entire oil output." You will learn about caulking and shade trees and showerheads and water-heater blankets.

❖ Why do we need it to be 78° in the winter, when it's cold outside, and 70° in the summer, when it's hot? **Reversing these two can save a heap of dough.** Ceiling fans can be a good investment—in the summer, obviously, but also gently rotating in the winter, to push the hot air back down to your toes.

❖ A **solar water heater** can be a good investment in some areas.

❖ A **"pool blanket"** costs next to nothing but, properly used, can add ten degrees to the temperature of your swimming pool and save a fortune compared with a heater.

• **Stagger your tax deductions.** A lot of people find each year that they have almost enough deductions to make itemizing worthwhile—but not quite. If you fit this category, or if you have barely enough deductions to itemize and thus save very little by doing so, consider bunching your deductions into every second year. Plan to itemize in 2000 and 2002, for example, but to take the standard deduction in 1999 and 2001. *Don't* make the year-end charitable gifts you normally would in 1999—make them in January 2000. (Likewise, local tax payments, medical payments, and any other potential deductions you may be able to push into 2000.) Come December 2000, *do* make your charitable contributions, prepay local taxes, and so forth. In half the years, you'll have the same standard deduction you would have had anyway. But in the other half you might find yourself with an extra $2,000 or $3,000 in deductions. That will save you $600 to $900 every second year, if you're in the 30% tax bracket.

• **Prepare your *own* taxes.** If you've been paying $100 or more to do your taxes, do 'em yourself and save all that money. Easier than you think. See pages 115–16.

• **Dial your *own* phone.** When you call information (already expensive, if a phone book is handy), you're now frequently told that the number you requested can be dialed *for* you for 35 cents. Just "Press one or say YES." Well, hey: I like Space Age marvels as much as the next guy, but spending 35 cents to save 10 seconds is paying a machine $126 an hour to do something you really could manage on your own.

• **Trim your *own* hair.** ("And tuck in your shirt," advises Mom. "*Look* at you!") You can have your hair cut every three weeks at $25 a clip—$425 a year—or you can get one of those stainless-steel razor-blade haircutting doohickeys and save, over five years, $2,125 plus maybe 100 hours of getting to, sitting in, and returning from the barber's chair. Or have it cut professionally a few times a year and do it yourself the rest.

• **Avoid buying lottery tickets** with your spare dollar at the checkout counter. They pay out barely 50 cents in prizes for every dollar sucked in; but since all the big prizes are heavily taxed, the odds are even worse. Heads you win 30 cents, tails you lose $1.

- Subscribe to *Consumer Reports* (800-234-1645), with its unbiased reports on virtually everything. Getting good value saves money.

- **When booking a hotel room, bargain.** "Gee, maybe I should check your competition—don't you have a cheaper rate?" This sometimes turns one up. Even better may be to call a consolidator like Hotel Reservations Network (800-634-6835), which buys blocks of rooms at rock-bottom rates and then resells them to you and me.

- **Another place to bargain: credit cards.** If yours charges an annual fee, call to see whether it will match the cards that don't. Often they will. It's cheaper for them than replacing you. Meanwhile, if you have more than three cards, you have too many—especially if you're paying annual fees to own them. Sure, it makes sense to have one in a safe place, in reserve, in case your wallet gets stolen* or there's some billing dispute or computer snafu with your primary card. But six or eight cards? And department store cards? Why?

Two extra cards it *may* profit you to carry:

The Transmedia Card saves 20% at selected restaurants on all but the tax and tip. Call 800-422-5090 or visit www.transmediacard.com to sign up. Along with your card, you'll get a directory of participating restaurants. If you choose to eat at one, simply hand the waiter your card when the check comes. He gets his full tip, so you won't detect even the subtlest condescension when he thanks you for your patronage. At month's end, you'll see two things on your Visa or MasterCard or Discover bill (whichever you authorized Transmedia to charge): all your restaurant charges, as usual; but, on a separate line, your 20% credit. So if you take your spouse to a romantic $50 dinner (plus tax and tip), you'll see a $10 credit. Romance each other

---

* Quick tip: photocopy the contents of your wallet. In case it ever *does* get stolen, you'll be glad you did.

once *every* week at participating restaurants and you save $500 a year. Go with five colleagues to a $100 lunch (plus tax and tip), and you'll see a $20 rebate on your next credit card statement—even if your company reimburses you, or your fellow diners insist on passing $20 bills to the head of the table. (Presumably, you'd pass the savings along to them.) If you don't live in one of the areas the card currently covers, it could still be worth carrying for that occasional business trip or vacation.

The **IGT Charge Card** offers 25% so long as you pay your bill on time. IGT (In Good Taste) includes hundreds of restaurants Transmedia does not, so broaden your options and carry both. You'll get discounts at hotels and resorts from England to the Caribbean and Hawaii, and on everything from flowers to eyeglasses to dry cleaning to limo service to parking. Call 800-444-8872 or visit www.igtcard.com to sign up.

The discounts these cards offer is possible because a lot of decent restaurants have excess capacity, and—just like airlines that would rather sell seats cheap than see them go empty—are willing to sell meals "wholesale." (The economics of restaurants and airplanes aren't actually much different. Restaurants are just slower.) Transmedia and IGT get an even bigger discount off the price of the meal, so the more you eat, the more they make. For the restaurant, it's a way to attract new customers and fill empty seats. The discount becomes a form of highly targeted advertising. Instead of giving the money to a radio station to get you to come, they give it to *you*.

Just remember that it's still a lot cheaper to have Pepsi and pasta at home.

• **Quit smoking.** At a pack a day, there's $1,000 a year right there. Tell your teenager you don't care about her health or her soon-to-yellow teeth, you care about her *money*. The decision to develop a saving rather than a smoking habit makes a huge difference. One way, she puts $1,000 a year into Marlboros and, at age 65, has cancer.

The other way, she puts it into a mutual fund that compounds at 12% a year and, at 65, has $2.4 million.*

• **Buy the store brand.** Private-label merchandise is often made on the same production line, with the same ingredients, as the more-expensive advertised brands. Aspirin is aspirin, no matter how elaborate the commercials get.† Bleach is bleach. It is a sad fact of American consumer patterns that poor people in particular avoid private-label brands, despite the potential savings—so persuasive is national advertising. For example, private-label shaving cream is occasionally on sale at $1.09. Believe me, it works just as well as the name brands on the next shelf that sell for $2.39.

Granted, not all private-label merchandise is as good as its name-brand competition. None of it, presumably, is better. You will never find *me* eating a ketchup other than Heinz. But is it really worth 80% more to you to sneeze into a genuine Kleenex-brand "kleenex"?

• **Ice water** has at least as much nutritional value as Diet Coke, and it's free. Drinking lots of water is supposed to be good for you.

• Scotch drinkers can tell one scotch from another, but show me the man who can tell what **vodka** was used to make his vodka tonic. If status symbols are important to you, buy *one* bottle of Absolut and a 59-cent plastic funnel. It should last a lifetime.

---

* Smokers also spend more on life insurance, cold remedies, and health care. The Tobacco Institute may even now not be convinced smoking kills, but the three life insurers *owned* by tobacco companies certainly are. All three charge smokers about double for term insurance. Meanwhile, a division of Dow Chemical found that smokers averaged 5.5 more days of absence each year and took 8 more days of disability leave.

† *Consumer Reports* is devastating in comparing such brands as Bayer, Bufferin, Anacin, and Excedrin with plain private-label aspirin. The difference is almost entirely in price, with here and there some caffeine or a trace of antacid or an aspirin-like analgesic thrown in. At one store, they found a 100-tablet bottle of generic aspirin for 99 cents versus Bayer for $4.99.

- Call loved ones on weekends and at night. Better still: **e-mail.**

- We've already talked about Cepacol. **Consider buying** *services* **"by the case,"** too.

I got my flood insurance renewal notice recently and a choice: one year at $429 or three years for $1,147. Which would you choose?

It's the kind of choice we face frequently, perhaps most often with magazine subscriptions. Here's how you might go about making a rational decision:

In the example above, you're "investing" an extra $718 up front to save $140 (paying $1,147 instead of $429 three times—$1,287). But what kind of return is that?

The trick is to figure out how long you're tying up the money. Your first inclination may be to say "three years," but that's wrong. If you had paid annually instead of all at once, the second $429 would have been due just a year from now, so that portion of the $718—fully 60% of it— is only being tied up one year. And the rest ($289) is only being tied up two years.

If 60% of your $718 is being tied up for one year and 40% for two years, then the whole thing, taking a weighted average, is being tied up for 1.4 years. (How'd I get that? I multiplied 1 year by 60% and got .6 years; then multiplied 2 years by 40% and got .8 years; then added .6 and .8 years together to get 1.4 years.)

What kind of return is it to earn $140 on $718 in 1.4 years? If you're not into computers or higher math, just divide the $140 return by the $718 investment and you get a 19.5% gain. Divide *that* by 1.4 years and you get a wrong, but close, answer of 13.9% gain per year. The precise answer—easily obtained with a pocket calculator or computer program that includes "present value" functions—is 13.569%. And it's tax-free.

On top of that, there's the saving in time and expense of having to pay the bill each of the next two years. If you figure each payment costs you a buck in postage, materials, and effort, the saving climbs to $142. And there's the saving if, by locking in today's price, you avoid price increases in years two and three.

So the after-tax return offered on tying up your $718 may be even better than 13.5%.

On the other hand, you should consider whether there might be some cancellation fee if you decided to terminate your insurance (or magazine subscription) in mid-term, and whether the insurer (or magazine publisher, or health club, or exterminating service) might go broke before the end of the three years, leaving you uninsured (or with nothing to read, no place to work out, or rats).

If all this penny-pinching sounds niggling, don't miss the larger point: taken together, you can very likely save $1,000 a year—and possibly much more—with very little effort. And that's important, because the typical American doesn't save enough. When this book was first published, personal savings as a percentage of disposable income in the U.S. was 9%. For the last decade it's been *half* that.

Most people need to do better for themselves—and can.

CHAPTER 3

You CAN Get By on $165,000 a Year

A penny saved is—impossible.

—OGDEN NASH

Many of us spend a great deal of time worrying about our money; few of us use that time to make a sensible plan. Where am I? Where do I want to be? How do I get there?

If you already have a budget, or are too rich or frugal to need one, skip to page 46. But if like many successful people you have trouble making ends meet, let alone overlap, *listen up*. This is important, because it's not just a budget you'll end up with, it's an overall plan.

First, get a pencil and a yellow legal pad (or a computer and a piece of software like *Quicken*). Next, tell your secretary to hold your calls. If you are a secretary, get a smaller legal pad. If you neither are nor have a secretary—if you've got a *man's* job, like operating a crane—do this at home, in your favorite chair, late at night, when no one can see you. (Real men make bets, not budgets.)

If you have a significant other, sit him or her down, too, and work on this together.

1. **Tally your net worth.** Add up everything you own, subtract everything you owe, and that's your net worth.

   In other words, before you even start to make the budget, take a few minutes to see where you stand. Down the left side of the first sheet of your yellow legal pad, list all your assets and their approximate value— the house, the car, the savings account. Down the right, list all your debts—the mortgage and car loan and credit-card balances. Which list totals more?

If you own more than you owe, you have a positive net worth. You're already three steps ahead of the game.

If you have a negative net worth—you owe more than you own—you can see why your mother is worried about you. (What's that? You think just because she passed away she's not worried?)

Subtract what you owe from what you own and write the total at the bottom of the page.

2. **Set goals.** Where would you like to be a year from now? "Out of debt" might be an appropriate goal. And two years from now? "Out of debt with $2,000 in an IRA and $2,500 in the bank and a stereo system that will wake up the dead." And five years from now? "A net worth of $60,000 headed for half a million."

It is to reach these goals that you make your budget. Write them down on the second page of your yellow legal pad. Don't make them too aggressive. Try to set goals that, after going back and forth with your budget for a while, you secretly think you'll be able to exceed. If you aim too high, you'll never feel you're doing well enough. You can still have unwritten goals and hopes and dreams—by all means!—but think of them (and not too often, if you can help it) as icing on the cake. Sure you want a Porsche. Everybody seems to want one (not me—I want to be invisible and to fly). But it's really nuts to want one so much you're unhappy you don't have one.

3. **Figure your annual earnings.** At the top of the third yellow page, list all your sources of annual income: your take-home pay (multiply your paycheck by the 12, 24, 26, or 52 times a year you receive it), payments from Grandpa's trust, the $20 a week you pick up reffing Little League, dividends, and so on.

Note that for most folks, it's not a long list. "Take-home pay: $28,400." End of list.

Note also:

❖ Precision is not the goal. Ballpark estimates are fine.

❖ When in doubt, estimate low. That way, any surprises are likely to be pleasant ones.

4. **Take a first pass at your expenses.** This is like naming all the states. If you picture the map and start with Maine, gradually working your way south and west, you will come up with 43 states. Then you'll remember Kansas (if you're from Kansas, you'll remember Delaware) and a few others and get to 48. The last two are murder, though you know them perfectly well (Nebraska—of course! Alabama!), and you may even have to sneak a look at the map to find them.

So it goes with budget categories. You'll quickly come up with headings to cover most of your expenditures, although with budget categories, unlike states, there are no preset boundaries. You might have one broad category for Entertainment or several narrower categories all summing to it: Restaurants, Movies & Tapes, Books & Magazines, Theatrical & Sporting Events. Whatever makes sense for you.

Nor is there a specific number of budget items the way there's a specific number of states, so you won't know with quite the same certainty whether you've missed any. You'll *think* you've thought of everything, just as, until you count up your list of states, you think you've hit them all. But chances are, you have not. (Gasoline—of course! Lawn Care!) If you get stuck, sneak a look at the map—last year's checkbook and credit-card statements. Under what headings would last year's expenditures have fallen? (Miscellaneous! Of course!)

Next to each category, estimate what you currently spend. If you haven't any idea what you currently spend—well, all the more reason to be going through this exercise. Two nights out a week at $75 apiece? (Not hard to do, between dinner, a movie, and ice cream on the way home.) That's $7,800 a year.

Some categories, like this one, are best thought of in weekly terms and multiplied by 52. Your rent or mortgage payments and electric bill are naturally thought of in monthly amounts and multiplied by 12. Your semi-annual trips to the dentist are multiplied by two—but don't include them at all if you're reimbursed for dental care by insurance. Reimbursable expenditures don't affect your financial plan, so ignore them.

Ignore, too, items that are automatically taken out of your pay, because it was only your net take-home pay that you listed as income. Or, if you prefer, list your *gross* pay as income and list each of the deductions—taxes, health insurance, and so on—as an expense item. Either approach is fine.

Don't include Credit Cards as a budget category. Only the annual credit-card fee itself and, more important, credit-card interest ought to be budget items. The rest—the clothing and dinners and such you charge to the cards—should go into categories like "Clothing" and "Dinners."

On your first pass, jot down both the annual expenditure and the way you figured it ("$75 2/wk = $7,800"). Make no effort to economize. When in doubt, estimate high. Round up. Your auto insurance runs $950? Call it $1,000.

Leave for the end of your list those "expenditures" that aren't really expenditures at all: investments. The $2,000 you voluntarily contribute to an IRA is not like the $2,000 you blow on a Carnival Cruise. It's cash that merely moves from your front pocket to your back pocket. Similarly, spending $40,000 on an Oriental rug, if it's really worth $40,000 (as the ones that fly clearly are), isn't spending money at all. It's merely shifting funds from one investment, like a savings account, to another, like a rug. (If the rug would fetch only $25,000 were you immediately to resell it, then you have in effect invested $25,000 in a rug and spent $15,000 on your living room.)

If you buy a new car every four years, for cash, don't budget zero for the first three and then $18,000 for the fourth. Budget $4,500 a year (plus maintenance, plus insurance).

If you own your home, include an allowance for maintenance and repairs even though you can't be sure what might need fixing or when. If you budget $2,500 a year, planning to repaint, but the roof starts to leak— well, this year you might patch the roof and, if funds are scarce, hold off repainting until next year.

5. **Take a second pass at your expenses.** What have you forgotten? Furniture? Appliances? Gifts? Inevitably you'll think of other things as you go along, but that's why you do this in pencil.

6. **Refine your plan.** Add up your expenditures, not counting things that are really investments, like IRA contributions. How does what you expect to shell out compare with what you expect to rake in? Ideally, you're raking more than you're shelling, and by enough to meet the goals you've set for yourself on the second page of this legal pad. Usually, though, you're not.

   What's the shortfall? Are you living a $50,000 life-style on a $45,000 income?

   You have three ways to close the gap:

   ❖ Spend less.

   ❖ Earn more.

   ❖ Set less-aggressive goals.

   Go back over your budget and, without being unrealistic, see what you can trim. ("There are several ways to apportion family income," counseled Robert Benchley, "all of them unsatisfactory.") Before, scrimping this way was a chore. Now it's still a chore, but a chore that's part of a grand plan.

So first trim your budget. But don't trim it unrealistically. Don't set yourself up to fail.

Then, if your expenditures and goals for saving still exceed your income, think about increasing your income.

Sadly, this often involves doing more work. But if you don't already work two jobs or live rent-free by acting as super for your building or drive a cab on weekends or wait tables or type term papers—and if you want to achieve your goals and work less hard in the future—you should consider it. For one thing, you'll earn more money. For another, you'll spend less. You'll be too busy and tired to spend.

If you can't get or don't want more work, take yet another pass through your expenses—but a radical one this time. You could, for example, move to a cheaper home. You could give up skiing for jogging or take in a roommate.

Your other choice is simply to set lower goals.

Round and round you go, juggling income, expenses, and goals, brushing eraser nubble to all corners of your kitchen table, until you arrive at an earning-spending-saving plan that adds up. The process itself is useful. It helps you set priorities. It helps you see where your finances are headed and, if you like, redirect them. What's involved here, really, is taking control of your life.

By estimating your income low and your expenses high, you set yourself up to succeed. That makes your budget a game that's fun to play instead of a constant burden of guilt and discouragement you'll soon abandon.

(Speaking of discouragement, if you've got three small kids, don't be discouraged that you're unable to save much. For many, it's only before the kids are born and after they've graduated that any serious saving is possible. But even just funding an IRA as they're growing up, though hard, can put you $250,000 or $500,000 ahead of the game in your later years. So try to set *something* aside.)

In setting your goals, spend a little time thinking about the things you have (like your health, and a $359 25-inch Sharp color TV with remote control) and not just the things you don't (a personal trainer and a $2,995 60-inch Matsushita).

7. **Blow $5 on a budget book.** Once you've settled on a plan, buy a simple budget book at any stationery store to track your progress (or a small computer—see below). It doesn't much matter what method you choose, so long as you use it. Nor need you wait until January to start. The government budgets on a fiscal year; so can you. Most budget books are set up to record 12 months' expenditures but let you fill in the names of the months. The first can be April just as easily as January.

8. **Keep track of what you spend—or choose an altogether different system.** Before you go to bed each night, enter the day's expenditures. To help remember what you spent, save your receipts and carry a three-by-five card in your wallet to jot down the rest. Indeed, budget or no budget, you'll likely reduce expenditures that make you feel foolish when you have to write them down.

Is all this too tedious for words? Here's a simpler system: Destroy all your credit cards. Deposit the first 20% of each paycheck in one or more investment accounts that you never, ever touch (the "don't-touch-it budget," as budget counselor Betty Madden calls it). Put the remaining 80% in a single checking account and make do, no matter what, with the balance in that account.

It's an unconventional financial discipline, but better than the Visa budget system most people use. Under that system, Visa tells you exactly what you can afford to spend (your available credit) and exactly how much to pay each month (your minimum monthly payment), all the while collecting 15% or 20% for its trouble.

9. **Give yourself a break.** If you do take the time to plan your financial future and to track your progress as it unfolds, don't be slavish about it. Who cares if you forget to jot down every last expense? Who cares if you go over budget from time to time? The idea isn't to account for every penny (although it could be an intriguing experiment for three months to see exactly where the money goes). The idea is to spend less than you earn each year, get out of debt, and build a secure, comfortable future.

   The trick is to live a little beneath your means, motivated by the carrot (saving up in great anticipation of whatever it is you're saving up for) rather than the stick (having to pay for it—even though it wound up raining the whole time you were there).*

   Living beneath your means is tough. (Living *within* your means is tough!) Making a game of it helps. Seeing it as a challenge helps. "Paying yourself first" helps (direct the first 10% or 20% of every paycheck to a savings account or mutual fund). But tough as it is, as you begin to see results, it gets easier. And if you want to get ahead of the game, you're more likely to succeed this way than by buying lottery tickets each week.

   One way or another, the future will come. With a little planning, you can have a say in how it looks. Think of your budget not as your albatross, but as your secret weapon.

Doing It by Computer

Since you have to pay your bills somehow, there's much to be said for doing it by computer. Whether you use *Quicken*

---

* "I bought a dress on the installment plan [runs the old ditty]. The reason, of course, was to please a man. The dress is worn, the man is gone—but the dang installments go on and on."

or *Microsoft Money* or some other software program, once you get set up you'll save lots of time and "capture" the data you need to print reports, prepare your taxes, and track your budget.

For example, here's how I pay my mortgage each month: I don't. It's paid automatically, through a service called CheckFree. Every month the payment is debited from my bank account and credited to the mortgage company. When my interest rate changes, a few keystrokes in *Managing Your Money* tell CheckFree the new amount. Meanwhile, the program keeps track of each month's interest payment (for preparing my taxes) and principal (for adjusting my balance sheet as the equity in my home grows).

For the Florida Power & Light bill, which varies each month, I just click my mouse a couple of times and enter the amount. Everything else is filled in for me. No need to write a check, along with my account number and the "amount in English" ("two hundred seventy-nine and 14/100" dollars). No need to find a stamp. This payment, and whatever others I've entered equally fast, gets transmitted over the phone to CheckFree, which makes the payments five business days later.

Of course, you can print checks too (or write them by hand and enter them later). But the beauty of all this is that the information, once entered, is retained. Want a quick list of all the times you've paid the hardware store, if there's a dispute? Bang—it's there. Want to compare what you've spent on clothes this year with last? Bang. Want to reconcile your checkbook quickly and easily? Bang.

And each year, personal finance software programs get better. Many offer direct connections to your own bank account, so you can actually "see" your account status at any time, without having to wait for your statement, and do at home everything you might at an Automatic Teller Machine. "Except get cash," people used to snicker—but even that may change. True, you won't be able to print your own greenbacks. But by the time you read this, or shortly thereafter, the banks and software companies will have begun experimenting with "cash" cards. Swipe your card through a little machine at the store, and that $1.99 burger is paid for—with $1.99 deducted from the "cash" on your card. To replenish it, you'd just boot up your software, hook into the bank, and electronically order $200 transferred from your checking or savings account to your cash card.

The advantage of the computer is that it makes budgeting, and tracking your budget, *fun*. It puts you in control of your finances. You become chairman of the board. Where before you had no convenient way to track your finances throughout the year, now it's all kept track of *for* you. Personal finance software has been credited with saving more than one marriage.

Obviously, a $500 or $1,000 expenditure on a computer to do this can take quite a whack out of your budget all by itself, so I'm not suggesting you join the computer revolution for this reason alone. Indeed, one day not far off all this may be possible right through your TV. But if you do have a computer and aren't using it to pay your bills and prepare your taxes . . . to make a budget and then track your progress . . . you're missing something good.

Getting By on $165,000 a Year

Most of us feel we couldn't get by on a penny less. But all a family struggling to get by on $190,000 a year need do is look down the street to see a family that—somehow—manages to get by on $165,000 a year. (They do their own pool maintenance.) A family struggling on $24,000 need only look down the street to see one surviving—don't ask me how—on $18,500.

The point is that you *can* save money if you're willing to make some sacrifices. And it's wise to do so. Because even forgetting retirement needs, "rainy days," and all that, if you can only arrange things to come out a little ahead each year instead of falling a little further behind, you will quickly find your financial security and, not long afterwards, your standard of living improving. Money *does* make money. The rich *do* get richer. And they sleep better.

A lot of people manage to dig themselves into a big hole of debt. Some go bankrupt; most just muddle through life, juggling their bills and praying that an unexpected expense or job loss doesn't put their finances over the edge.

But there are success stories. One fellow I know of managed to pull back from a lifestyle that peaked at nearly $70,000 in credit-card debt—substantially more than a year's take-home pay—and he did it without bankruptcy.

Here's how he did it:

(1) Not having the heart to cut up all his credit cards, he just cut up one (which was at its limit anyway). Every day, he looked in the mirror and said, "Today, I will cut up another credit card." Although most days he couldn't bring himself actually to do it, a month of incantations finally got him down to the one card he felt he had to keep, for identification and business use. (A heavy debtor starts solving his problems when he just stops adding new debts. The members of Debtors Anonymous—which has local chapters throughout the country—are taught to take the same one-day-at-a-time approach as alcoholics, simply resolving not to borrow any money today.)

(2) He paid only the minimum monthly payments on his cards, but (and this was the key) he didn't rack up any *new* debt. So, gradually, he paid them all off. At the same time, he put just $50 a month into the stock market, via a mutual fund.

It might have made more sense, mathematically, to apply that $50 to paying off more debt, "earning" 18% tax-free by doing so. But psychologically, he wanted to start building something, however small. And he found that he didn't really miss that $50. He still felt broke all the time, he said—"but no broker." So he raised the contribution to $100 per month, then $150. As one credit card after another got paid off, his monthly debt payments decreased and his monthly investments increased. After five years he was saving 20% of every paycheck. And still does. He now has an investment portfolio that dwarfs his former debts.

If you have reached the point where late payments or even bankruptcy are considerations, check your phone book for the Consumer Credit Counseling Service, a nonprofit organization created in 1951 to assist debtors in getting control of their finances. There are a lot of disreputable operations that prey on debtors, but this organization, sponsored by many of the largest creditor groups in the country and usually charging little or nothing for its advice, acts as a go-between to arrange debt moratoriums, repayment plans, reduced payments, or interest waivers.

Consider the words offered to Charles Dickens by his father, a financial failure (words Dickens later put into the mouth of another financial failure, Mr. Micawber, in *David Copperfield*): "Annual income, twenty pounds; annual expenditure, nineteen pounds; result, happiness. Annual income, twenty pounds; annual expenditure, twenty-one pounds; result, misery." That's pretty much it. Spend less than you earn. Live a little *beneath* your means.

Saving is difficult, but less so when you have a goal and a plan. To sacrifice any given night on the town makes little sense. What's another sixty bucks? But as part of a plan to pay off all consumer loans within the year or build a net worth of $25,000 in five, a sacrifice that would otherwise seem pointless—even depressing—can be purposeful indeed. Satisfying, even.

No one wants to pass up something because he can't afford it. But to pass it up because he *wants* to—because his eye is on a higher goal—well, that is quite a different thing.

The day your paycheck comes, put 10% or 20% of it, automatically, without question, into a separate savings vehicle. It can be a savings account or a mutual fund or an IRA or some combination of accounts—but do it. (Your employer may be able to do this for you, which is ideal, because the best way to avoid temptation is never to see the cash in the first place.) Simply live as if you are making

$18,000 instead of $20,000; $45,000 instead of $50,000; $135,000 instead of $150,000.

There are loads of competent financial planners to help you make sense of your finances. But until you internalize the plan, whether you worked it out with a 79-cent legal pad or a $2,500 financial planner, it won't mean anything. You've got to make it *your* plan, and you're not likely to if you simply rely on someone else once a year to work it out for you. Buying fancy exercise equipment is fine, but it's not enough. You've got to *pedal*.

As with any regimen, the hardest part is getting into the habit. As your pile mounts, it becomes much easier.

But what to do with your pile?

CHAPTER 4

Trust No One

Trust everybody, but cut the cards.

—FINLEY PETER DUNNE

If you or anyone you know is over fifty, *I urge* you to get pencil and paper ready."

So begin the celebrity life insurance commercials you may have seen on TV. Dick Van Dyke's done them. Ed McMahon's done them. Even Gavin MacLeod—good ol' Murray on the *Mary Tyler Moore Show,* remember him?— has done them.

Murray, Murray, Murray.

But the plans sound good, don't they? No matter how bad your health, *you cannot be turned down* for this "top-quality, big-dollar" protection. Yet amazing as it seems— well, this is why I told you to get your pencil and paper ready—Murray's plan cost just $5 a month. And—get this!—your premiums were guaranteed never to rise as you got older.

Said Murray: "I can't tell you what a relief it is to know that we won't be a burden on our children." Here the kids thought they stood to inherit a pretty penny—Murray did go on to captain the *Love Boat,* after all—but had it not been for this insurance, they'd have been left with nothing but the funeral bill. *Thank heavens for this insurance.*

If you're 50, Murray said, just $5 a month would buy you $10,000 in protection.

Catch #1: If you died of an illness, your heirs got $2,800, not $10,000. The bulk of the insurance benefit was for *accidental* death only. Yet accidents are a minor cause of death among older people. (Dick Van Dyke's pitch called them "one of the leading causes of death for people over forty-five." But actually, fewer than 3% of deaths among people over 45 are caused by accidents. So more than 97% of the time the payoff would be $2,800, not $10,000.)

It was true, you couldn't be turned down for this coverage; but—Catch #2—only after you'd paid premiums for two years were you actually covered. Die of an illness before then, and your heirs got nothing but a refund of the premiums you had paid.

True, too, your rates were guaranteed not to rise (well, sort of) but—Catch #3—as you got older, your coverage would fall. Say you paid $5 a month, month after month, for 25 years. Then, at 75, having paid in a total of $1,500, you had a heart attack and died. This policy paid your heirs a grand total of $225. Period. (Die after age 79 and they got no benefit at all.) This is what Murray endorsed as BIG-DOLLAR protection. He couldn't tell you what a relief it was to know that $225 would be there when his loved ones needed it.

If at age 79 you died not of an illness but, say, hang gliding into a utility pole, your heirs would get an extra $775, except that—Catch #4—death while hang gliding didn't qualify for the accidental death bonus. Neither did death in a war (declared or undeclared), in a private plane, by suicide, during surgery, or while intoxicated, if intoxication caused the accident. (If you were merely three sheets to the wind in the bar car of your commuter train when it derailed and flew off a cliff, you'd be okay.)

Catch #5: Your rates were guaranteed never to rise *only so long as the insurance company didn't raise them*. They couldn't single you out and raise just your rate. But if the company decided *everybody* should pay $6 a month instead of $5, or to cancel all the policies altogether because it wasn't making money on them, the company was free to do so.

Catch #6: Five bucks a month was the least you could pay; but this was portrayed as *such* a good deal for "folks like us," as Murray put it—you know, warm, bald guys who make $80,000 an episode—that many folks signed up for the full $40-a-month's worth, to cover both them and their spouses four times over. Five dollars a month is nothing. But $40 a month, in the budgets of many older Americans—$480 a year—is a hefty sum.

The pitchmen freely acknowledge they're paid to endorse these insurance plans, but Dick Van Dyke said, in his follow-up letter: "P.S. I'm sure you know I would never speak out for anything I didn't personally believe in." Gavin MacLeod, in *his* P.S., wrote: "I want you to know I would never speak out for anything I didn't believe in with my whole heart." The cash Continental American Life paid him to endorse this plan had nothing to do with it.*

Trust no one. It kills me to say that, and I'll admit there are exceptions—but the list is shorter than you think. I mean, my God: if you can't trust *Murray!* If you can't trust the *Beardstown Ladies!*†

Here is an ad for a mutual fund. It comes from a well-regarded investment firm, and this is its *special* fund. In

---

* MacLeod and Van Dyke were both reportedly paid $25,000 to do the television commercials I refer to, plus a commission on each toll-free call the commercials produced. An executive close to the arrangement estimated the final take for each man to have been between $100,000 and $200,000.

† You mean you hadn't heard? These sweet, sweet ladies, who became world famous for their down-home recipes and shrewd stock-picking—who sold millions of books up through 1998 and made hundreds of TV appearances based on their extraordinary market-beating performance—turn out to have been calculating their results funny. Say you or I started the year with $40,000, added $5,000 more, and saw our account total $50,000 by year's end. You and I might say our $45,000 had grown very nicely to $50,000. About 11%. Not bad. What the Ladies apparently were figuring is that they started with $40,000, now it's $50,000—that's a 25% increase for the year. So instead of beating the market all those years, it turned out that—though sweet—they hadn't done particularly well at all. As the late Roseanne Roseannadanna would have said, "Oh! That's different! . . . Never mind."

fact, says the ad, this fund has appreciated at a rate of 21.5% a year for the last 10 years. Compare *that* with what your local bank is paying. You're smart enough to know performance like that can't necessarily be repeated (if only you had thought to invest 10 years ago!). And you imagine, given that they're trying pretty hard to sell this to you, there may be a sales commission involved (there is: only $4,575 of the $5,000 you were thinking of investing actually goes to work for you—the rest is an immediate loss). But never mind that. We're talking about 21.5% annual growth— enough, if it continued for another two decades, to turn a single $2,000 IRA contribution into $90,000!

You are all set to send in your money, when you come across Jane Bryant Quinn's column in *Newsweek*. She has studied the prospectus—you could have studied it, too, but you would have been a rare investor if you did—and she has noticed that the big gains that the fund packs into its alluring yield of 21.5% came long ago. In the first six of those ten years, share values rose an average of 39% a year. But zigzag performance the last four brought an average annual *loss*.

No place in the ad do you see anything about an average annual loss. And guess what? In the hot stock market ever since (this ad actually appeared many years ago, giving us, by now, the benefit of hindsight), the fund did grow smartly—but underperformed the monkey throwing darts.

Trust no one. You've got to take responsibility for your own affairs.

Many people wish they could turn the whole mess over to someone else. Widows particularly express this wish, having in some cases been made to feel over many years of marriage that they can't possibly understand anything having to do with money. But the folks who do understand money, while many have your best interests at heart, have their own interests at heart, too. You have to take responsibility for your own money because no one cares about it as much as you. That doesn't mean you can't rely on a variety of experts to help—a good accountant, a good mutual fund manager, perhaps a good real estate or insurance agent, financial planner or attorney. But ultimately it's you who is in charge.

If you don't understand what you're investing in, or haven't formed a broad spending/borrowing/saving/insuring/investing plan yourself, it's unlikely things will work out terribly well. (Most people wind up with nothing, says financial advisor Venita Van Caspel, "not because they plan to fail, but because they fail to plan.") What's more, you *can* do it. The simple investments are very often the best. And that goes, too, for the simple loans, the simple insurance, and the simple financial plans.

(I had a friend who earned $2 million a year at Merrill Lynch executing a very complex, computer-assisted trading strategy. Around 1990, he went out on his own and offered me and others the chance to do it with him. He labored mightily to explain exactly *what* he was doing, but all any of us could understand—even the head of an investment bank who also went in on this—was that a 50% annual gain was essentially guaranteed unless interest rates rose or fell more than 700 basis points in a single year. Which never happens—and didn't. Don't you wish you could get into deals like this? Don't you wish you knew what basis points are?* It was the most sophisticated, complex deal I've ever invested in. It sure wasn't available to "the Little Guy." And it lost money. Big time. My friend wasn't trying to fleece us. He meant well. He was just wrong—for reasons I could understand no better than what it was he was doing in the first place.)

It's not enough to respond to advertising headlines or the salesperson's enthusiasm or the lavishly illustrated brochure. You've got to read between the lines—or at least read the prospectus. And since you won't—most prospectuses

---

* Each basis point equals one-hundredth of 1%. When the prime rises from 7% to 8% it's climbed "100 basis points."

are unreadable—you've got to stick to sensible investments recommended by competent, disinterested parties. Not competent *or* disinterested, competent *and* disinterested—which certainly leaves out Murray, may very likely leave out tips from your hairstylist, and may even leave out advice from your accountant or financial planner, who could be getting a commission for steering you into a particular deal. ("Your purpose," a well-known San Francisco financial planner was quoted in the *Wall Street Journal* as having told a group of fellow financial planners, "is to get up before [potential clients] and confuse them. And step two is to create a dependency." Step three, in many cases, is to start selling them things.)

If only you had access to an expert you could *trust*. Someone who did know how to read a prospectus.

With that in mind, pour yourself a beer and get out your letter opener, for what we have here—delivered by hand to our door—is a fat manila envelope from nothing less than the United States Trust Company, one of the oldest, classiest, most exclusive banks in the country. ("When you do something very well," its ads say, "you simply cannot do it for everyone.")

Inside is everything you'll need to evaluate and sign up for the Samson Properties 1985-A Drilling Program. U.S. Trust—which actually *is* a very fine institution, this ancient episode notwithstanding—describes Samson 1985-A as "a quality oil and gas investment with relatively moderate risk, inherent tax benefits, and the potential for significant upside economic gains." (As opposed, one presumes, to downside economic gains.)

The bank's cover letter outlines the deal and encloses a colorful Samson sales brochure, a deadly 165-page Samson prospectus, a huge U.S. Trust business reply envelope for your signed papers, and a form you sign agreeing to pay the bank a 5% "advisory fee" for bringing the deal to your attention. (There is already a 7.5% sales commission built into the deal, but the bank can't touch it—it's illegal for banks to sell securities like these—so, instead, it charges this 5% advisory fee. The bank's not *selling* anything—merely sending sales materials, recommending that you buy it, and enclosing all the papers you need to sign to send in with your check. See the difference?)

By paying the "advisory fee," you are in effect getting the deal at 105% of retail. You could avoid the fee by purchasing Samson units directly through a stockbroker, but when you deal with a classy bank—this is not a bank that's out hawking car loans—you should show a little class yourself.

Participations in Samson 1985-A run $25,000 and up.

THESE ARE SPECULATIVE SECURITIES AND INVOLVE A HIGH DEGREE OF RISK, cautions the front page of the prospectus. The SEC makes 'em say stuff like that. The bank prefers to describe it as "relatively moderate risk."

The brochure explains that by mid-1984, "Samson's 1973–1981 Programs had distributed cash equal to 127% of total cash invested" and would distribute a further 226% over the life of those programs. The brochure says you shouldn't count on future programs all doing so well, but, hey, 127% and 226%—that's like three and a half times your money! Plus, U.S. Trust likes the program, and Samson must be getting more experienced each year, and drilling costs *are* really low these days, and boy, could I ever use the tax deduction—where do I sign?

At least that was my reaction.

The brochure did say, "These figures assume an equal investment in each of the programs offered from 1973 through 1981," but that sounds innocuous enough.

It turns out that its very first program, a teeny-tiny deal in 1973 that involved a total of just $325,000 and 11 investors, has paid off like gangbusters. But all its subsequent programs, ranging from 3 to 30 times as big, have mostly tanked. (Funny how often that first deal, which helps sell all subsequent deals, is a lot more successful than the rest.)

If you don't assume "an equal investment in each of the programs," but assume instead the amounts that were *actually* invested, the return on those 1973–81 programs by mid-1984 would have been not 127% (all your money back and then some), but 45% (less than half your money back).

Of the nearly $30 million that investors handed Samson in 1981 (not to mention the $70 million in 1982, 1983, and the first part of 1984), less than $1 million had been paid back by September 30, 1984.

Of the three 1980 deals—one private, two public—one had paid back 74%, two had paid 17% and 9% respectively. Guess which one was the private deal.

And understand, these numbers are not return *on* investment (with luck, that comes later), they're return *of* investment.

If there were a cynic in the room—and I trust there's not—he might suggest that Samson raised $100 million in drilling investments from 1981 through 1984 on the strength of one crummy little $325,000 program it had drilled ten years earlier.

In fact, I eventually discovered, *that first deal wasn't drilled by Samson at all*. It was drilled by May Petroleum. Samson merely purchased the producing wells at $2-a-barrel-era oil prices and kept pumping as oil prices shot sky-high, apparently realizing that it had the makings of a great brochure.

Having said all this, it's important to be clear that there are many drilling deals whose records are at least as uninspired (I've been in several) and that Samson's 1973–81 programs still have a lot of hydrocarbons in the ground. The brochure said that those programs were projected to return yet a further 226% of investors' money.

But what were these projections based on? What was Samson figuring, and U.S. Trust apparently buying, as a reasonable projection for the price of that oil still in the ground?

Right there on page 78 of the prospectus, paragraph 3, was your answer, plain as day. The 226% return yet to come was based not only on the fabulous results of that first teeny-tiny program Samson didn't drill, but also on the assumption that oil would continue to sell for $29.50 a barrel through 1986 (it actually dropped to $10 at one point) and then climb, over the following sixteen years, by 2002 to $75.

One of the nice things about going through the bank was that you got the benefit of its independent analysis. "In addition to the information contained in the enclosed Offering Prospectus, supplied by [Samson]," wrote the bank in its cover letter, "certain other facts should be made known to you."

Oh, boy, I thought: the dirt.

"In particular, our analysis has established [Samson's competence and its track record]." Whereupon the bank simply restated the assertion of Samson's brochure: "through June 30, 1984, Samson's 1973–1981 programs have distributed cash equal to 127% of total cash invested and had estimated future cash distributions equal to 226% of cash invested."

Somebody at U.S. Trust should have read the prospectus.

Yet if you can't blindly rely on U.S. Trust in such matters—truly one of the finest fiduciary institutions in the country, to which I owe a *lot* of money—on whom *can* you blindly rely?

No one.

CHAPTER **5**

The Case for Cowardice

This broker calls his customer for four straight years and each year puts him into some dreadful stock that drops right through the floor. The fifth year, the customer calls the broker and says, "Look: I don't know about all these stocks we've been buying— I think maybe I'd be better off in bonds."

"Yeah, sure," says the broker—"but what do I know about bonds?"

—OLD JOKE

I went to the track for the first (and last) time in my life some years ago. I went with a fellow who's been going twice a week since 1959. This is a man who knows horses. I know absolutely nothing about horses, but I brought $100 and figured I'd learn. About the only part I really understood were the hot dogs and beer, but the hot dogs weren't running and my midweek afternoon limit is three beers, so by the sixth race I was getting bored and decided it was time to place a bet.

My friend showed me the lineup for the race, explained why So-and-So would almost surely win, and just snorted when I said, no, I wasn't going to put my money on So-and-So, I was going to put my money on Willow. *Willow?* Willow, he chided, had never even raced before and had absolutely nothing going for her. (Or him. I never did get that straight.) She was the kind of horse they put in the race so none of the other horses would feel bad. "You're missing the point," I explained. "Willow is going off at 25 to 1."

My friend tried to tell me about sucker bets (the odds at the track are always against you, but they're against you worst on the long shots), but I went and placed my bet and came back to our box and began trying to figure out where the race was going to start from. All the races had been starting from different points on the track, and I had been having some difficulty training my rented binoculars on the proper stretch of grass.

"And they're off!" announced the stationmaster (I recognized his voice from the Penn Station P.A. system), and I'm asking—"Where?"

Even after I found them I couldn't really tell the horses apart, but according to the stationmaster, *Willow was in the lead*. I looked over at my friend, who had a knowing and slightly bored pucker to his face, and then back to try to find the horses. And Willow, according to the voice, *was still in the lead*.

I am ordinarily rather quiet among 15,000 strangers, but I had, after all, put my money on this horse, and I had, after all, consumed three fairly large beers. I began to shout, "Come onnnn, WILLow!" And Willow, at the half (or whatever they call it), was *still* in the lead.

Now, you think I'm going to tell you that with just a few yards to go, or furloughs or fathoms or something, Willow stumbled, or Willow punked out, or Willow got kicked by one of the other horses. But no—Willow won!

At 25 to 1, Willow won!

Unfortunately, I had bet only $3 of my $100 on Willow.

The point of all this—and I think you know it instinctively, but I'll spell it out anyway—is that if I had bet the full $100 on Willow, Willow would surely have lost. There is no way in the world she would have won.

Is there anyone who doubts this? Think about it.

People say, "One great speculation is worth a lifetime of prudent investing"—a terrific line, and true. The problem comes in finding the great speculation. Few people ever do, particularly if they are amateurs.

The line I prefer: "In the financial marketplace, you get what you pay for, if you're careful. If you try to get more, you get burned."

Savings accounts and money-market funds are for the chickenhearted. But I respect the right to be chicken-hearted. As you can perhaps tell from my Belmont stakes, I am rather chickenhearted myself.

The challenge of chickenhearted investing isn't deciding where to put your money, but resisting the temptation to put it elsewhere. *Face it: sure things are boring.* Treasury bills have terribly predictable plots that make lousy cocktail party conversation (even if they do have some redeeming snob appeal), and they won't make you rich. If the United States Treasurer really wanted to sell those bills, she would issue them at slightly lower interest rates—and put the dif-ference into a kitty for which there would be a daily draw-ing. The United States Lottery. That would give Treasury bill buyers something to check in the paper every day and a chance—however thin—to strike it rich.

Once in a long while you do find a sure thing with an outsized payoff, but it is very rare. The only time I was ever so fortunate was decades ago, with a stock called Nation Wide Nursing Centers. Of course, under normal circum-stances nursing home stocks are not fare for the chicken-hearted. But this was one of those rare sure things. Through some remarkable good luck, on a day when this stock was selling for $22 a share over-the-counter—that was the price *you* would have paid—*I* was able to snag 500 shares at just $8 each "under-the-counter." The only hitch was that the shares were unregistered, which meant I couldn't sell them for a while. It was a virtual gift of $7,000, which was hard enough to believe, let alone turn down.

Ordinarily, however, there is no such thing as a financial bargain. The financial markets are too large and efficient for that. By and large, as I've said, if you're careful, you get what you pay for. Try to get more and you generally get what's coming to you. I was told I would have to hold my nursing home stock for three months, when it would almost surely be bought out by a merger-mad steel company at $40 a share. The head of research for one of Wall Street's most prestigious firms was in the deal for 4,000 shares, so I knew this was on the up-and-up.

The stock went to zero in under a year.

There are two kinds of money in the world, debt and equity. (I find this easy to remember, because that's what a friend named his two golden retrievers: Debt and Equity.) Debt is an IOU; equity is a piece of the action. Debt is bonds or bills or CDs—anything where you *lend* your money, whether to the U.S. government, a local government, a savings bank, a corporation—whomever. (Yes, when you deposit money in a savings bank, you are actually lending money. The bank is in your debt and must pay you interest. You have taken their IOU in exchange for your cash.) Equity is where you *invest* your money, with no promise that your investment will be recouped, but with the idea that as the company prospereth or falleth into decline, so shall you prosper or fall. (Actually, it's not that simple. The company may prosper while its stock falls. But we'll get to that.)

A very basic thing to know about your money is that, over the really long run, people who buy equities—stocks— will almost surely make a lot more money (if they're at all sensible in how they do it) than people who make "safer" investments. Unfortunately, people tend to focus on this crucial fact and give it real credence only when the market is hitting record highs, losing faith when it's in the dumps, leading them to buy high and sell low. But it's true all the same. Especially when the market has tanked—a sorry condition that can last many years—*never lose sight of this basic fact.*

Yet until you have at least $5,000 or $10,000 someplace safe and liquid, like a savings account—unless you are so wealthy you don't have to worry about the contingencies of everyday living—you are crazy even to consider making riskier investments. Or more sophisticated ones. Relax: You are doing the right thing. You are *not* a sap. There is a time and place for everything, and when cocktail party conversation turns to "investments" or "the market," I suggest the time has come for you to be smug. Let the others do what they do, say what they say—you are above it. They may gamble, they may speculate, they may talk of doubling their money (and not mention halving it); you are smug. (See pages 219–20 for a set of smug rejoinders and harmless financial one-liners to keep up your end of the conversation.)

The television campaign the savings bank people used to run about commercial banks being for businesses, while savings banks are for people—"and I'm a people"—is so silly as not to bear discussion. But the other one you may have seen, which shows a man recounting his sad history of investment failures, and then has him brightening to say that now his money is in a savings account—he's "found a better way"—that one may be equally simpleminded, but it's really not such bad advice. The first several thousand dollars of anybody's money (aside from equity in a home) should be in a checking or savings account (or a money-market mutual fund, which is essentially the same thing). And for many people, that's *all* their money.

In choosing among savings accounts that provide checks and checking accounts that pay interest (and money-market funds that do both but are not federally insured), the important thing to remember is: It doesn't make much difference.

By and large, the going rate for safe, liquid funds will be about the same everywhere. One bank may offer a bit more than another for a while; money-market funds usually offer a bit more interest but entail a tiny bit more risk and may be a little less convenient (and downright uncomprehending if you ever go to them asking for a home-improvement loan); credit unions may offer a slightly better deal because they are nonprofit.

But essentially, you just want your account, or accounts, someplace convenient that provides good service. (There's something to be said for doing much or all of your banking business with one institution in order to build a good relationship.)

The danger is that you will spend so much time trying to figure out whether the 5% savings account with the $4 monthly fee but no charge for checks is a better deal than the 4.5% checking account with no fee but a 25-cent charge for each check or deposit (answer: choose the one with the closest cash machine) that you will lose sight of the larger issues. For the real question is not how to wring an extra 1% out of the $5,000 or $10,000 you keep completely safe and liquid. An extra 1% on $5,000 or $10,000 comes to $50 or $100 a year—after taxes, even less. You are too busy to spend much time worrying about $50. The real question is overall strategy: What proportion of your assets do you want to keep completely safe and liquid? What proportion might you prudently tie up for a while to get a higher return? What proportion should you risk in the stock market to get a higher return still? What proportion should be in tax-free securities? Or in real estate? How well are you diversified?

The book that really used to get me, back in the days when all any small saver could earn was 5½%, no matter what, and no saver of any size had even dreamed of double-digit rates, was the one that promised to tell you "HOW TO MAKE UP TO 13% OR MORE ON YOUR SAVINGS— ALL FULLY INSURED!" It went on to say how upset the savings banks were about this book, but there was nothing they could do, and the interest you earned could be even more than 13%, etc., etc. And when you sent for the book— could you really have expected differently?—you found that to earn these astounding rates of interest you had to spend most of your waking life transferring money with split-second precision from one bank on a Friday afternoon to another that handled its accounting a different

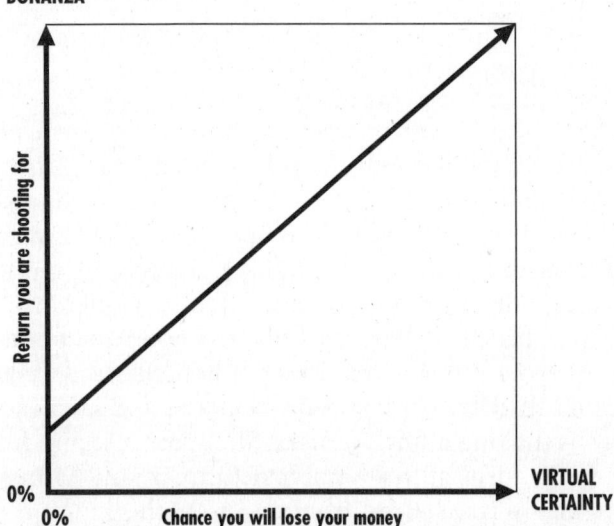

Basically, you want a fund that's convenient and that has the lowest possible annual expense charges. The less they charge, the more you get to keep.

The most convenient money-market funds for substantial investors are the cash-management accounts—CMAs—offered by most brokers. Here your cash balances are automatically swept into a money-market checking account. And if you overdraw your cash balance, it triggers an automatic, relatively low-cost margin loan against the value of your stocks and bonds.

Safe as money-market funds are, whenever you venture beyond FDIC-insured bank accounts you ought to try to understand what you're investing in. Thousands of investors in the Piper Jaffray Institutional Government Income Portfolio (how's that for a safe-sounding name?) found out they had lost nearly 30% of their money in a few months in 1994 because it had reached for a higher yield by speculating on interest rates. Several other money-market and short-term government-bond funds were saved from disaster only by large infusions of cash from their parent firms.

Treasury Bills

The safest short-term securities in the world are United States Treasury bills. And the formerly daunting $10,000 minimum purchase amount has, happily, been reduced to $1,000. T-bills are fine for a competitive yield on money you'll want to have available in three months, six months, or one year (the three maturities the Treasury offers).

You can purchase Treasury bills (and notes and bonds—read on) from any Federal Reserve branch via a Federal program called Treasury Direct. Purchases and sales can be as easy as making a phone call or filling out a secure Internet website form at **www.publicdebt.treas.gov.** Money is automatically transferred from and to a checking or savings account you specify. You can also give standing instructions to reinvest ("roll over") your bills as they come due. If you need to sell early, you can do that, too. The Treasury will get you a competitive bid and handle the sale for a nominal fee.

Treasury bills don't pay interest in the normal way. Instead, they are sold at a discount. (The exact amount of the discount depends on an auction process you don't need to participate in.) Say you send in $10,000. The discount is credited to your bank account shortly after the bidding. It's like getting your interest in advance. The $10,000 face value arrives at the end of the holding period (unless you ask for the bill to be rolled over and reinvested). If you purchase a one-year Treasury bill with a $10,000 face amount and a 5% discount, you will receive $500 immediately, so that the net cost of the bill is only $9,500. Your interest rate is equal to the $500 discount divided by the $9,500 effective cost, or 5.26%. It's not taxed until the bill matures. And Treasury interest is never subject to state or local income taxes.

Treasury bills trade on the open market, so you can buy and sell them *after* they are issued, bypassing Treasury Direct. But this involves paying a commission in most cases. Your bank or broker will be happy to oblige.

LONG TERM

When you buy a bond you are lending money, whether to Uncle Sam, General Motors, or the City of Houston. There are three risks. The first is that you won't get paid back. The second is that you'll get paid back early. The third is that, should you want to sell the bond sometime before maturity (the payback date), you won't be able to get as much as you paid.

The first risk is a function of the creditworthiness of the borrower. It could go broke.

Happily, you need not spend more than a few minutes investigating the creditworthiness of the entities whose bonds you are considering. This is done *for* you. Every major bond is rated by two rating services, Standard & Poor's and Moody's. *Their* men in green eyeshades pore over balance sheets and coverage ratios and footnotes—and reduce it all for you to school grades. Triple-A (AAA) is the best. Anything with a B in it (Baa, for example) means "Beware"; it is probably OK, except this is the chapter about taking minimal risk and sleeping soundly at night, so stick to A-rated, or even double-A-rated, bonds. (C-rated bonds are pure speculations.)

The folks at the rating services are not infallible, but their analyses are likely to be as astute as yours or mine, so why waste time duplicating their effort?

Even without checking the ratings, you can tell a lot about the quality of a bond just by looking at how its yield compares with the yields of other bonds. These are reasonably "efficient" markets, and you just are not going to find one safe bond that is way out of line with the rest. If anything, you should shy away from bonds that pay exceptional interest: there is a reason they pay so well.

And because the future is unpredictable, even for monoliths like the phone company, it is only prudent to diversify. Don't lend all your money to Pacific Bell—a breakthrough in mental telepathy could ruin you. Spread your money around.

Yet it doesn't pay to spread your money over *too* many different bonds, because the flip side of diversification is volume. Bonds are denominated in $1,000s,* but any order for fewer than 25 at a time is like buying the travel-size toothpaste: you really get nicked on the price.

The second thing to watch out for in buying a bond is its "callability." Many bonds are issued with provisions that allow the issuer to call them in before maturity. When this happens, you get the full $1,000 face value of the bond—often with a small premium—but then have to go out looking for a new place to lend your money. And since borrowers have a tendency to call their bonds when interest rates have fallen—just as you might refinance your mortgage—you may be sorry you didn't buy a noncallable bond.

One way around this is to buy bonds that, though callable, were issued when interest rates were lower, and so sell in the open market at a discount. If you buy a bond for $680 and it's called away from you ten years early at $1,000—well, I can think of worse things, can't you? (When the general level of interest rates is low, you won't find bonds selling at deep discounts. Sorry.)

The third risk in buying bonds is that you may lose money when you go to sell them—even though if you held on to maturity you would get the full $1,000 face value. That's because: **When interest rates go up, bond prices go down.**

---

* Don't be confused by the way they are quoted—as a percentage of par ($1,000). A bond selling at 88¼—88¼% of par—costs $882.50; at 94½, $945.00; at 106⅜, $1,063.75.

There is a market for money just as there is a market for everything else—coffee, plywood, lemons—and when lots of people are trying to borrow but few are willing to lend, the price (namely, interest rates) goes up. When few are trying to borrow and many are eager to lend, the price (interest rates) goes down. Simple supply and demand, plus a good dose of government intervention. (The government controls the overall supply of money—which unlike coffee, plywood, or lemons does not grow on trees.)

The key to everything financial, and to nearly everything economic, is interest rates. When the going rate for money rises, bond prices automatically (and stock prices almost as automatically) fall. When the going rate for money falls, bonds (and stocks) rise. There is nothing mysterious about this; it is simple arithmetic. If you paid $1,000 ("par") for a bond that paid $50 a year interest, and then interest rates went up such that newly issued bonds were paying $70 interest, who in his right mind would buy yours for $1,000? Why would anyone take 5% interest when the going rate had risen to 7%? If, however, you offered the bond at, say, $850, you might be able to sell it (depending on how long it had to run to maturity), because the buyer would be getting $50 interest on $850—5.88%—plus the prospect of a $150 profit when the bond matured.

It's like a seesaw. Rates up, bonds down. Rates down, bonds up. It's just two ways of expressing the same thing, like the fullness or emptiness of a glass.

(On stock prices, interest rates have a triple-barreled effect. For one thing, the higher interest rates go, the less attractive stock dividends look by comparison . . . so people sell stocks to buy bonds, and stock prices fall until dividends do look attractive. Second, high interest rates discourage people from borrowing to buy stocks on margin. Third, high interest rates mean high costs to business, a drag on consumption and, often, lower profits. It's possible for stocks to rise despite rising interest rates, or to fall despite falling interest rates, just as it's possible air conditioner sales could rise in a summer that's a degree or two cooler. The "seesaw" is not completely automatic, as it is with bonds. But it's an extremely powerful relationship nonetheless.)

There are different interest rates for different kinds of borrowers and different kinds of loans, but they all move in rough tandem. If the rate banks charge their prime customers goes up, you can be sure the rates they charge their lesser customers will go up as well. If corporations have to pay more interest to float a bond issue, you can be sure municipalities do, too.

Interest rates, furthermore, sit on top of inflation. If inflation is generally expected to run at 6% a year, lenders are going to feel awfully foolish lending their money at 5%—so they don't. As a general rule of thumb, long-term interest rates on high-quality bonds run around 3% above lenders' expectations of long-term inflation rates.

For a bit of perspective, let alone nostalgia, see on the facing page how interest rates have fluctuated since 1920.

You will notice that someone who bought a 20-year 3% bond at face value ($1,000) when it was issued in 1955, entitling him to $30-a-year interest until 1975, probably began to feel regretful around 1957, when similar bonds were being issued at nearly 4%—$40-a-year interest. It is the same feeling one would have buying a TV set shortly before a greatly improved model was released.

Had one, on the other hand, bought some 6% General Motors Acceptance Corp bonds at $430 each in July 1982— bonds that promised to pay a paltry $60 a year until 2011 and thus sold for less than half their $1,000 face value— one could have turned around and sold them in January 1983 for $560 apiece. A 30% gain in six months.

Clearly, if you knew which way interest rates were headed, you could profit in numerous ways. Many people therefore try to guess, and some, in any given year, guess right. Few, however, can guess right consistently, least of all you or I or the man on all-news radio. Experts disagree; and the majority view at any given time is about as likely to be wrong as the minority view. The one thing on which

A Table That Looks Boring But Is Actually Most Revealing

Year	Prime Rate	Triple-A Bonds	Municipal Bonds	Savings Accounts	Home Mortgages	Inflation
1920	6.58%	6.12%	4.98%	4 %	5.75%	2.3%
1925	4.98	4.88	4.09	4	5.90	3.8
1929	6.02	4.73	4.27	4½	5.92	0
1930	3.50	4.55	4.07	4½	5.95	−6.0
1935	1.50	3.60	2.40	2½	5.26	3
1940	1.50	2.84	2.50	2	5.40	.1
1945	1.50	2.62	1.67	1½	4.70	2.3
1950	2.07	2.62	1.98	2	4.95	5.8
1955	3.16	3.06	2.53	2¾	5.18	4
1956	3.77	3.36	2.93	2¾	5.19	2.9
1957	4.20	3.89	3.60	3	5.42	3.0
1958	3.83	3.79	3.56	3¼	5.58	1.8
1959	4.48	4.38	3.95	3¼	5.71	1.5
1960	4.82	4.41	3.73	3½	5.85	1.5
1961	4.50	4.35	3.46	3½	5.87	.7
1962	4.50	4.33	3.18	4	5.90	1.2
1963	4.50	4.26	3.23	4	5.84	1.6
1964	4.50	4.40	3.22	4	5.78	1.2
1965	4.54	4.49	3.27	4	5.74	1.9
1966	5.62	5.13	3.82	4	6.14	3.4
1967	5.63	5.51	3.98	4	6.33	3.0
1968	6.28	6.18	4.51	4	6.83	4.7
1969	7.95	7.03	5.81	4	7.66	6.1
1970	7.91	8.04	6.50	4¼	8.27	5.5
1971	5.70	7.39	5.70	4¼	7.59	3.4
1972	5.25	7.21	5.27	4¼	7.45	3.4
1973	8.02	7.44	5.18	5	7.95	8.8
1974	10.80	8.57	6.09	5¼	8.92	12.2
1975	7.86	8.83	6.89	5¼	8.75	7.0
1976	6.83	8.44	6.64	5¼	8.90	4.8
1977	6.82	8.20	5.68	5¼	8.68	6.5
1978	9.06	8.99	6.03	5¼	7.92	9.3
1979	12.67	10.05	6.52	5½	10.94	13.0
1980	15.27	12.77	8.60	5½	13.50	11.9
1981	18.87	14.17	11.23	5½	14.70	8.9
1982	14.86	13.79	11.57	5½	15.14	3.9
1983	10.79	12.04	9.47	5½	12.57	3.8
1984	12.04	12.71	10.15	5½	12.38	4.0
1985	9.93	11.37	9.18	5½	11.55	3.8
1986	8.33	9.02	7.38	5½	10.17	1.1
1987	8.21	9.38	7.73	5½	9.31	4.4
1988	9.32	9.71	7.76	5½	9.19	4.4
1989	10.87	9.26	7.24	5½	10.13	4.7
1990	10.01	9.32	7.25	5½	10.05	6.1
1991	8.46	8.77	6.89	4½	9.32	3.1
1992	6.25	8.14	6.41	2½	8.24	2.9
1993	6.00	7.22	5.63	2	7.20	2.8
1994	7.15	7.97	6.19	2	7.49	2.7
1995	8.83	7.59	5.95	2	7.87	2.5
1996	8.27	7.37	6.75	2	7.80	3.3
1997	8.44	7.27	5.55	2	7.71	1.7
1998	8.5	6.5	5.2	2	6.9	1.7

there is nearly unanimous agreement is the difficulty of predicting interest rates.

Certainly rates in the fifties seemed very high by comparison to those in the forties—yet in the sixties they climbed still higher. Almost no one in the world would have believed, in 1965, that a mere 15 years later interest rates would top 20% in the United States of America—which is why they were willing to buy long-term bonds that yielded less than 5%. I like to think we may not see such lofty rates again in our lifetimes. But by the time you read this—or by the next time you do—rates could be even higher. Or spiraling inflation could shatter the value of the currency altogether, as it did in Germany after World War I, in which case any long-term fixed-income security becomes worthless. On the other hand, imagine how great you'd feel if you had bought 15% Treasury bonds in 1981, as many brave souls did.

We have become increasingly aware in this country that inflation of much more than 2% or 3%—or certainly 5%—is murderous. It drives up interest rates, eats away at profits, lowers living standards, stifles the incentive to invest, worsens unemployment. Runaway "double-digit" inflation is the economic equivalent of nuclear disaster, a thing that must be avoided at all costs—or so most economists and politicians believe—if the economic order is to survive. As a result, one expects a great deal of effort and energy to be applied at the highest levels to keep interest rates from reaching new peaks.

This was not nearly so much the case in the fifties and early sixties, when the rise in inflation and interest rates, though unwelcome, was not widely perceived to threaten the foundation of society. It was thought, in fact, that a bit of inflation was a good thing. It made everyone feel prosperous—wages and profits and real estate values kept edging up—and the confidence *that* inspired helped to keep the economy bubbling along. But if inflation of 2% and long-term interest rates of 5% are well within the system's tolerance, double-digit inflation is something else entirely. In 30 years, $1 shrinks in buying power to 54 cents at 2% inflation. But at 12% inflation it shrinks to 3 cents.

The prospect of $1 shrinking in value to 3 cents in 30 years so threatens prosperity that central bankers and even politicians are likely to try hard to keep inflation in check.

So much for background. What sorts of long-term chickenhearted investments should you consider?

Treasury Notes

These are "intermediate-term" bonds, issued with lives between two and ten years. They compare nicely with CDs you'd get at your bank, especially because the interest they pay is exempt from state and local income taxes. Like Treasury bills, they can be bought through the Treasury Direct program. The minimum purchase is now just $1,000 as with T-bills. But instead of selling at a discount, like bills, Treasury notes are regular bonds, issued for $1,000 and paying interest semi-annually.

Once issued, Treasury notes trade actively, so you can easily buy or sell them any time. Unlike bank CDs, there's no penalty for selling early, other than the commission you pay your bank or broker. Because of the interest-rate seesaw, you'll make a profit on your notes if interest rates have declined since you bought them, or suffer a loss if rates have risen. (A nice twist here, often overlooked, is that Treasury notes tend to rise in value slightly as time goes by; so if you do sell early, you're not likely to suffer a loss. Why? Well, remember that the market generally pays more interest for a longer-term loan than a shorter one. And remember that as time goes by, the Treasury note you bought has a shorter and shorter remaining life. Someone thinking of buying your note doesn't think of it as the 5-year note you originally bought; he thinks of it as a 2-year note, if that's how long it has left until maturity. When he sees that *your* "2-year" Treasury pays $60 a year interest when those currently being issued pay only $50, he'll pay a little extra for yours.)

Treasury Bonds

Treasury bonds are the third leg of the Treasury triangle—bills, notes, and bonds—which at the end of 1998 came to about $5.5 trillion in all. This is the famous "national debt" you've read so much about. It's owed to the owners of these bills, notes, and bonds. You, perhaps.

Treasury bonds are the same as Treasury notes, only with maturities in excess of 10 years. Generally speaking, you shouldn't buy them, because over such long periods you'll nearly always do better to invest in stocks. Furthermore, 10-year notes typically have a yield almost identical to 30-year Treasury bonds, so you're not being rewarded to risk your money for those extra 20 years. (And the Treasury note twist described above does not apply. Because rates don't drop appreciably as you go from 30 down to 10 years, there's no natural tendency for bond prices to rise slightly as those 20 years inch by.) If inflation kicks up, the value of your bonds could plunge if you went to sell them early . . . or, if you actually held them the full 30 years to maturity, you'd find that, because of inflation, their $1,000 face value wouldn't buy much.

True, if interest rates are high and you lock them in for 30 years, you could make a good profit when rates fell back down. (That seesaw again.) But it's very hard to predict the direction of interest rates; and falling rates could make stocks go up even more than bonds. Only in a Depression-type deflationary situation would Treasury bonds outperform the stock market for long periods of time. So think of long-term Treasuries as a Depression hedge.

Stocks are perceived to be riskier than bonds—and over relatively short periods of time (and especially if you don't spread your risk by diversifying) they certainly are. But after inflation, someone who remained continually invested in long-term Treasury bonds from 1946 to 1981 would have had an overall loss of 70%, even before considering taxes. After taxes, the loss would have been closer to 80%. It's true that after 1981 bonds then turned around, finally, to score a huge gain. But they still didn't equal the performance of the stock market over the same period. The Dow Jones Industrial Average bottomed at 777 in 1982. Sixteen years later—not even counting dividends—it had more than tentupled. So you would have done well locking in high bond yields when interest rates peaked, but far better buying stocks.

Inflation-Adjusted Bonds

The Treasury began offering long-term "inflation-indexed" notes in 1997 (and similar Series I—as in "Inflation"— savings bonds in 1998). They pay a fixed rate of interest over their term (currently 5 or 10 years), but their $1,000 face value actually rises with inflation (and falls with deflation—but not below $1,000). One big drawback: the IRS treats these semiannual inflation adjustments as taxable income, so you're paying tax each year on income you won't actually get until you sell the bonds or they mature. Ah, you say: then why not put them in my tax-deferred retirement account? OK—if you're 90. But if you still have a few decades ahead of you, these are an awfully conservative choice for long-term money.

Municipal Bonds

There are two kinds of bonds: most of them, which are taxable; and municipals, which are not. Interest on bonds issued by state and local governments or agencies (county sewage authorities and the like) is usually exempt from federal income tax—and from that state's local income taxes as well. Interest on New York City bonds, for example, is exempt from federal, state, and city income tax (but not from California or Illinois income tax). The higher your marginal tax bracket, the more sense it makes for you to favor tax-free bonds.* If you are in the 30% or 40% tax bracket and have taxable bonds in your closet, it's very hard to see why you shouldn't sell them and buy municipals instead. If you have to sell at a loss to do this, all the better. The loss will lower your taxes.

Municipal bonds are not as safe as Treasuries, but "general obligation" bonds—those backed by the full faith and credit of a state or local government, not just the revenues from a hospital or a toll road—are awfully safe. Even if a town gets in trouble, the state is likely to find a way to help keep it afloat, because if bondholders lost money it would raise the borrowing costs for all the *other* towns in the state (as bond buyers became warier) and perhaps for the state itself. You might be inconvenienced for a while—some New Yorkers in 1975 were forced to wait an extra year before their "one-year" notes paid off, though they got interest for that extra year—but even in a rare disaster, like Orange County's 1995 bankruptcy, you would likely recoup all, or nearly all, your investment.

Another risk to consider is the possibility that some day the tax-free status of municipals will be revoked. But even if municipals did lose their exemption—unlikely!—that would almost surely affect only newly issued bonds. In which case old municipals would likely *rise* in value, because there would be a limited and gradually shrinking supply.

A final risk: that income taxes will one day be abandoned for other forms of taxation, rendering the exemption worthless. Well, maybe. But something tells me that between revenue-hungry federal, state, and local governments, there will always be some advantage in owning tax-free bonds.

---

* You see a lot of ads saying that, to a guy or gal in the 40% marginal tax bracket, a 7% tax-free bond "is the equivalent of earning 11.66%." Nonsense. A 7% tax-free bond is the equivalent of earning 7%—and getting to keep it.

If you're buying or selling municipal bonds, always get at least two prices—one from your regular broker, if you have one, and one from a company like Gabriele, Hueglin & Cashman (800-422-7435) that specializes in municipals.

What a lot of people do is buy municipal-bond *funds*— a mistake. Sales and management fees cut deep. One popular marketer charges a 6.3% sales fee—so in effect the first year's interest all goes down the drain—plus an annual 0.67% management fee. That may not sound like much, but it can amount to 10% or more of your return. So it's probably better to do a little homework and buy munis directly, if you're rich enough to buy some at all.

Note: Gains you might make selling tax-free bonds at a profit (if the interest-rate seesaw has lifted their price since you bought them) are subject to capital-gains taxes like any other gains.

Corporate Bonds

Don't buy them. The safest ones, sometimes called investment-grade bonds, pay only a bit more interest than Treasury securities but are subject to state and local taxes. So it's a wash. What's more:

❖ You can buy Treasuries with no commission, through Treasury Direct.

❖ If you decide to sell, Treasuries are more liquid than corporate bonds, which means you'll take less of a haircut.

❖ If you decide *not* to sell, you won't have to worry about having your bonds called in early. Treasuries are non-callable.

❖ You won't have to worry about default. Sure, safe bonds are pretty safe. But what if the blue-chip company that issued them decides to borrow $10 billion to make some dumb acquisition that doesn't work out? Or what if it becomes someone else's dumb acquisition, and all its cash reserves are drained off by the acquiring company? Treasuries are *completely* safe.

Of course, you can find corporate bonds that pay much higher interest than Treasuries. The riskier the bond, the higher the interest you stand to earn. But ordinarily, if you believe in the issuing company, you might as well buy its stock and *really* profit from its success (and at lower capital-gains tax rates, to boot).

Junk Bonds

Bonds issued with particularly high yields are called "junk bonds" (though not by the companies that issue them). Never buy them when first issued because, as I've said, if they actually turn out to be OK, the underlying stocks will probably turn out even better. Why speculate when the most you can earn is 12% a year (if that's what the bond is issued to yield when safer bonds are yielding 9%)?

But sometimes junk bonds can be an interesting speculation. They promised to pay 12% interest when they were issued, but now times are tough, the interest payments have been suspended, and sellers are dumping them in a panic. The sellers could be right, of course: the bonds could prove totally worthless. But say you buy them at 50 cents on the dollar and worse does *not* come to worst. Now at least there's some real upside. That 12% coupon, if interest payments resume, means $120 a year on each bond you just snagged for $500—a 24% annual return. And if the interest payments do begin to look secure, the price of the bond will head back up toward $1,000, so you could make another fast 50% that way. But as lucrative as this can occasionally be, it's clearly not the stuff of chickenhearted investing. It's much more like buying a speculative stock—to which all the caveats in the following chapters apply.

Bond Funds

Nah. You get diversification and professional management—but why pay for something you don't need? Treasuries are already safe; you don't need to diversify. And, especially being free of local income taxes, their yield is already pretty good even without professional management.

The problem is that everyone involved in a fund, not unreasonably, wants to be paid for his work, and the brokers executing all the buys and sells want to be paid, too. When you buy a Treasury security direct from the Federal Reserve, with nobody else taking a cut, you are starting with an advantage that turns out to be too hard for most funds to overcome.

For convenience, a fund that just buys and holds investment-grade bonds and lets you write checks against it—and make contributions in odd amounts (unlike the Treasury)—may be worth considering. But pick a fund with no sales charge and VERY low annual expenses (even 0.5% per year is too high for a bond fund).

As for safety, you know by now you can't trust the word "government" in a bond fund's name. One telltale sign of most of the funds that have had problems: returns that consistently exceeded the competition with no reasonable explanation, such as lower annual expenses. Actually, lower expenses alone are a positive sign of safety, since a fund manager following an exotic and dangerous strategy probably expects to be paid more for all the extra work.

Unit Trusts

Unit trusts are bond mutual funds that are not managed. Whatever corporate or municipal bonds they start out with are the ones they keep. As a result, there is ordinarily no management fee to speak of. There is generally a sales commission, however—typically 4%. That's the killer. Imagine a savings bank that charged you a 4% fee to accept your money and only then began giving you interest on the $96 of each $100 that remained.

Unit trusts can be found advertised in the *Wall Street Journal,* and brokers will be more than eager to sell them to you. They are put together with different maturities, so you can choose one that suits you. They provide diversification; but some of the trusts will accept risks—such as hospital bonds backed solely by the revenue of the hospital (and not by the taxing power of the city or county it is located in)—that you yourself might not. The fella who assembles the package of bonds is more concerned that the yield look attractive, so it sells, than that 12 years from now, when he is in his hot tub on Maui, the bonds remain safe.

Once sold to the public, unit trusts are not traded. Investors may redeem their shares with the trustee at "net asset value"—at a loss if bond prices have fallen since the trust was issued, at a profit if they have risen. But if you sell early, the handicap of that up-front sales fee bites particularly deep.

Forget unit trusts.

Convertible Bonds

These pay a specified interest rate but also give you the right to convert your bonds into a given number of shares of common stock. That's what's known as an "equity kicker." With a convertible bond, you have a chance to both sleep and eat well. In tough times, unless the company goes bankrupt altogether, you still get your interest; but should the company strike it rich, you could profit along with the common shareholders.

Say some company's stock is selling for $25 a share. Now they need to raise some more money, so they issue 7% bonds (when others are paying 9%) *convertible into 30 shares of stock*. Their hope is that people will accept 7% interest because of that conversion feature. Of course, there's no point converting right away—you'd be trading a $1,000 bond for $750 worth of stock (30 shares at 25 each). But what if the stock hits 100? Wow!

The problems with this are: (a) few stocks climb from 25 to 100 all that fast; (b) if this one does, you would have made more money spending your $1,000 to buy *40* shares of stock; (c) if it's callable, it might be called away from you long before it hits 100.

This isn't to say convertible bonds are terrible investments. They can be fine. But why are you suddenly going to give up your other hobbies, or quality time with the kids, to become a convertible bond expert? As I have already argued, corporate bonds don't make a lot of sense—buy Treasuries if you want safe yield. And as I will shortly argue, picking individual stocks doesn't make sense for most people—the way to invest for stock-market appreciation is by investing in no-load mutual funds.

Next.

Zero-Coupon Bonds

Zero-coupon bonds pay no interest. Instead, they're sold cheap and rise gradually to $1,000 at maturity. The longer the maturity, the lower their price. Back when interest rates were sky-high, I bought one that sold for barely five cents on the dollar. What fun to see the $100,000 face value show up on my brokerage statement each month! Over the next 30 years, the market value of the bonds would rise from the $5,125 I paid to $100,000. That's a little better than 10% compounded.

Purchasers of ordinary long-term bonds may lock in high interest—but what will they earn in interest *on that?* That's the beauty of a zero-coupon bond: assuming the issuer doesn't go broke, the compounded annual return is locked in from the start.

Zeroes are far riskier than regular bonds, if you don't intend to hold them to maturity, because small swings in the prevailing long-term interest rate produce huge swings in the market value of the bonds. Think of that seesaw again. With zeroes, it's a huge one: 30 feet tall, say, and 30 feet from your seat to the fulcrum. At first, you (and your partner at the opposite end, 60 feet away) go way up and down. But if you both inch toward the center, a foot a year, then by the 29th year, almost nose to nose, neither one of you is going up or down very much. At its exact center, the seesaw doesn't rise or fall at all. To a 30-year zero-coupon bond, "the exact center" is the day of maturity, when—assuming the issuer can pay off (the seesaw hasn't been torn down to build a body-piercing salon)—it's worth exactly $1,000.

So you'd only want to consider a zero-coupon bond when interest rates are very high, and from an issuer you consider impregnable (if you're in this for safety).

Actually (even though this is the wrong chapter for it), it might be more interesting to speculate in zeroes of companies in precarious shape—but at such low prices that if they pulled through, you'd reap it. In the last revision of this book, I bragged about owning some Revlon Worldwide zeroes purchased in mid-1994 at 43 cents on the dollar and promising 100 cents on March 15, 1998. "If they pay off," wrote I—this is an anecdote without an ending, as yet—"I will have reaped a compounded annual 25% return. If they don't, I'll get somewhere between zero (if the issuer goes bankrupt and there are not enough assets to pay the bondholders anything) and more than that (if there are)." I took this gamble knowing nothing about Revlon Worldwide except that the guy who controls it, Ron Perelman, is a billionaire who'd be embarrassed if the bonds defaulted. (So it was a no-lose situation. Either I'd make a lot of money, or I'd get to feel superior to a billionaire.) As it turned out, they paid off. And yet, when—emboldened by this success—I tried to repeat it with Perelman-associated Marvel Toy bonds at 20 cents on the dollar, I lost virtually every penny. And I don't even feel all that superior.

The four other big caveats with zeroes (the first being that you could lose money):

- ❖ They're taxed. Never mind that you're getting no interest; says the IRS: if the bond is geared to appreciate at 10% a year, then, by golly, you're going to *pay tax* (ordinary income tax) as if you'd gotten 10% in interest. The two loop-holes: municipal zeroes (free of tax on this "imputed" interest, just like any other interest) and zeroes held within a retirement plan (see the next chapter).

❖ Many are callable. At first, this would not seem to be a problem. What sort of lunatic corporate treasurer, after all, would call in bonds at par ($1,000) that are selling at some tiny fraction thereof? But zeroes are callable not at par, but according to special "accretion schedules" outlined in their prospectuses. So instead of seeing your money compound at 8% a year for thirty years, the music might stop after just five or ten. Be sure to check the call provisions before you buy.

❖ Some zeroes trade fairly actively and are listed in the paper every day, but many do not. You'll always be able to sell, but you may not be offered the world's fairest price.

❖ Outside of a retirement plan, zeroes add to your tax preparation woes if you sell them—even municipal zeroes—because the IRS wants you to compare what you actually got from the sale with what you "should" have gotten based on the way your bond would gradually have risen from your purchase price to its eventual $1,000 face value. If you were ahead of the curve when you sold, and got more than would have been expected when you bought it, you pay capital gains tax on that extra. If you're behind the curve and got less, you get to take that as a capital loss.

Preferred Stocks

Preferred stocks are like bonds. You get a fixed payout each year but no piece of the action. They are "preferred" only in that their dividend must be paid in full before any dividend on common stock may be paid; and should the company fail, preferred shareholders come ahead of common shareholders—but behind an awful lot of others, such as bondholders—if anything remains to be split up. What preferreds do not provide is an opportunity to participate in the company's good fortune, should it have any. The dividend never goes up.

A "cumulative preferred" is one that promises to pay its dividend no matter what, even if it can't be paid on time. The dividend may be omitted if necessary, but it is still owed to the preferred stockholders, and no common-stock dividends may be paid until all the preferred dividends are brought current.

By and large, preferred stocks are not good investments for individuals. One reason is that corporate investors bid them up in price. To corporations, but not individuals, preferreds provide an important tax advantage. Why should you pay a premium for a tax break that doesn't apply to you?

Series EE Savings Bonds

Series EE savings bonds are different from normal bonds. They're not denominated in $1,000s, they don't send semi-annual interest checks, and they don't trade in the open market. When this book was first published, they may have been the worst savings vehicle in America. Now, for small savers, they're not bad.

Savings bonds started out as war bonds. Uncle Sam used love-of-country to get small savers to accept miserable rates of return. After Vietnam, Watergate, and the inflation of the 1970s, people were less eager to do this. As a result, two major changes were made:

❖ In 1982, the interest rate became competitive. For bonds issued after May 1, 1997, the rate is pegged to 90% of the 5-year Treasury rate. The value of the bonds is adjusted at the beginning of every month (though if you hold on for less than 5 years, you lose the last 3 months' growth by way of penalty). These rates compare very favorably to passbook savings accounts, especially since the interest is free of state and local taxes. (For today's rates, call 1-800-

US-BONDS or check the Treasury's website at www. publicdebt.treas.gov.)

❖ In 1990, Congress exempted them from federal tax as well, *if used to pay qualified higher education costs of the tax-payer, spouse, or a dependent.* This advantage is phased out for high-income taxpayers, but most families saving for college should qualify. You don't have to designate the bonds as being for college costs until they are redeemed, so you needn't wait till you have kids to start buying them (though you must be at least 24 years of age when you purchase a bond in order to get the exemption later on).

Otherwise, savings bond interest *is* subject to federal income tax. But you have the option of paying it as it accrues—which would make sense for a child or adult whose income is so low no tax is due—or deferring it until you actually redeem the bonds. (How do you pay tax each year when none is due? By filing a tax return declaring the income, and saving a copy of the return with your permanent papers.) In fact, not only can you defer the tax for up to 30 years, you can roll matured Series EE Bonds into Series HH "retirement" bonds, which pay a modest rate of semiannual interest. That interest is taxed, but the accumulated interest on the EEs continues to be deferred until the HHs are redeemed.

Savings bonds are a slow but steady way to build assets, designed to meet the needs of the smallest saver. They have face values between $50 and $10,000 and sell for exactly half that. How many banks will let you start a savings account with only $25—and with no maintenance fee! In fact, because they make no money on them, banks aren't crazy about savings bonds and have successfully lobbied Congress to limit any one person's purchases to $15,000 per calendar year ($30,000 face value). Even so, virtually any bank in the country has the forms for you to fill out to buy bonds, which will be mailed to you by the government within a few weeks of purchase.

Easier still, tens of thousands of employers offer payroll savings plans that deduct your purchase—one $50 bond (which costs $25) a week, say—direct from your paycheck.

When you do redeem bonds:

❖ Redeem the newest ones, to minimize taxation on accumulated interest, which will be greatest on the oldest bonds.

❖ But if you're using this money for tuition, and qualify for the tax exemption mentioned above, redeem the *oldest* bonds, to exempt as much interest as possible.

Fine point: The new inflation-indexed Series I savings bonds sell for their full face value, not half, allowing up to $30,000 a year in actual purchases. (The limit of $30,000 hasn't changed, but by selling these new bonds at face value, Congress sneaked through a doubling of the limit without the bank lobbyists noticing it. Or so it seems.)

Loans to Friends

"It is better to give than to lend," said British war correspondent Philip Gibbs, "and it costs about the same." A better solution may be to offer to guarantee a bank loan. You are still on the hook if your friend or relative defaults, but in the meantime the bank sends the nasty letters. What's more, the fear of a bad credit rating might actually do more to get the loan repaid than the fear of losing your friendship.

Two Final Words to the Chickenhearted

1. *Getting a high rate of interest doesn't help if you don't save money in the first place.* Many people won't save unless "forced" to. For this reason, a payroll-savings plan or some other form of modest-return saving (for years, savings bank Christmas Clubs paid no interest at all!) is better than *planning* to invest in something with a higher return and never getting around to it.

2. *It's important for us chickenhearted souls to understand true risk.* The biggest financial risk you face is not that you will suffer occasional losses on your investments. It is that you will not accumulate enough money to pay the important expenses that must come out of savings: unexpected emergencies, house down payments, college, retirement. Saving more money is the surest way to reduce this risk. But, especially for retirement, it probably isn't enough.

Even if you sock away 20% of every paycheck your entire adult life, you will only have enough to live on for about eight years, unless you get some growth. After taxes and inflation, it is virtually impossible to get it from debt instruments. That long-term growth will almost certainly have to come from exposure of some of your money to short-term uncertainty in equity investments: in stocks, rental real estate or perhaps your own business (or all three).

It is unlikely that you will be able to accept the uncertainty of these investments without having a base of savings that feels truly *safe.* Your own common sense tells you that trying to squeeze extra interest out of *safe* money is a sure way to expose it to risk. So don't feel dumb keeping your short-term money someplace truly safe and convenient, and exposing your long-term money to prudent risk.

Tax Strategies

A taxpayer is someone who doesn't have to take a civil service examination to work for the government.

                    —*Stock Trader's Almanac*

Taxes drag down your investment results.

Up until 1986, when the top federal tax bracket was 50%, people would, understandably, do almost anything to try to beat taxes. The world was awash with tax-shelter salesmen. But tax shelters, as it turned out, were generally a way to spend $20,000 to avoid $10,000 in taxes. Oil-and-gas deals, railcar deals, bull semen deals—I lost so much money! I never did a bull semen deal, but boy, did I do oil and gas. In Ohio, mostly, which may have been my first mistake.

Now much of that nonsense is gone—partly because the top tax brackets have come down, partly because people have learned from their mistakes, and partly because, along with lowering the top tax brackets, Congress closed a lot of loopholes.

Good. Most of them just led to stupid behavior anyway.

In this chapter: a few basic notions that can significantly reduce the drag of taxes on the growth of your assets.

Kids

The best advice, of course, financially, is not to have any. But if you've already ignored that—and I hope you have— one way to have some of your savings compound tax-free is to save money in *their* names, with *their* Social Security numbers on the savings or brokerage accounts, and let *them* pay taxes on the interest or dividends that accrue. As the tax code currently stands, there will be no tax due on the first $700 a child under 14 earns and only 15% due on the next $700, for a total of $105 in tax, versus perhaps $500 you might have had to pay yourself. (Beyond $1,400, the investment income a child under 14 earns is taxed at the parents' rate. From age 14 on, it's all taxed at the child's rate.) With two kids earning $1,400 a year each in dividends and interest, you'd save twice as much.

Each parent can give each child up to $10,000 each year without having to pay gift tax. (Actually, a little bit more—the number is now indexed to inflation each year.) As custodian of a child's savings or brokerage account, you have the right to withdraw funds at any time to spend on the child's behalf (except that if you use the income from the account for basic child support, the IRS may tax you as if you, not the child, had earned it). The child may not touch the money before turning 18 or 21, depending on your state, though you can relinquish custodianship sooner (or elect to keep control until age 25 in California, Nevada, and Alaska).

Say you had twins tomorrow and saved $1,000 a year for 18 years for each of them. Say, further, that you could grow their money at 7% after tax in your tax bracket, but at 9% after tax in theirs. After 18 years, you'd have cleared an extra $14,600 by saving it in their names.

There are drawbacks:

- ❖ It complicates your life, having to keep track of this and file a tax return for each child each year.
- ❖ The money you save this way *belongs to your child*. He or she might decide to spend it on pernition rather than tuition when the time comes.*
- ❖ When the time does come, financial aid officers will be less generous to a child with $40,000 in blue chips than to a

---

* Pernition: not a word, but ought to be.

pauper whose parents have that same $40,000 augmenting their retirement fund. This is a moot point if you are fairly well off, since your child will not likely get outright scholarship money either way. Loans are the aid that will be available, and their availability should not be jeopardized by your child's nest egg.

Perhaps the best reason to save some money in your children's names is to get them interested. You might even choose to set up some sort of "matching" program where for every dollar your son or daughter saves from her babysitting or computer-consulting fees—or even just from her allowance—you'll kick in an extra buck or two. Not that you want to turn your 13-year-old into a middle-aged Midas, complaining about the double taxation of dividends while her classmates are complaining about homework. But instilling good money habits—like smart shopping and steady saving—is one of the best things you can do for your kids.

Education IRAs

The misnamed Education "IRA" is not a form of individual retirement account (unless you're planning to live off your well-educated children)—and unfortunately not much of an educational savings program, either, although there's talk of improving it.

Currently, an Education IRA may be established in the name of any child. Anyone can make nondeductible contributions to it (not just the child or parents) until the beneficiary reaches 18. After that, all the money may be withdrawn tax-free to pay for higher education costs. If little Sally has decided to join the circus instead of the Class of '08, the money can be rolled into the plan of her baby brother, or else just sit there growing, in case trapeze turns out not to be Sally's calling and she decides to go to college after all. If money is still in the account when the benefici-

ary reaches 30, it will all be distributed to the beneficiary and its growth subjected to ordinary taxes and a 10% penalty.

Only $500 per year can be contributed on behalf of any one beneficiary—much ado about practically nothing—and Congress included a provision that denies a taxpayer the HOPE Scholarship Credit in any year in which funds are withdrawn from the Education IRA. Since that would amount to $1,500 in most cases, it is extremely unlikely that the benefits of IRA tax exemption will overcome the loss of the HOPE Scholarship tax credit. Better to save your $500 chunks directly in the child's name, as just described.

In the spirit of the grotesquely complex 1997 Tax Simplification Act, there was soon talk of amending the Education IRA to make it more appealing. If you've already set one up—swell. There's certainly no harm in it, and Congress might one day even make them worth doing.

In any event, funding retirement plans such as 401(k) plans, Keoghs, and true IRAs should definitely take priority over Education IRAs, especially where those plans permit early withdrawals for education.

Retirement Plans

As you doubtless know, the money you've been paying in Social Security taxes, lo these many years, has not been set aside for your retirement. Most of it has been paid out to people already in retirement (e.g., your parents or grandparents). It's gone. In my view (see the Appendix for details), Social Security will always provide at least bare subsistence for those in need. But if we want to retire in comfort, we will have to provide, in large measure, for ourselves. Fortunately, there are a variety of tax-deferred retirement plans to help.

The best retirement plans are the 401(k) and 403(b) "salary-reduction plans" that tens of millions of employees contribute to. What makes them so good is that many employers add 25 cents or 50 cents or even more to each dollar you choose to save this way. *This is free money.* If your employer offers a deal like this and you're not taking full advantage of it, you're an idiot. (Well, I'm sorry, but c'mon: if your local bank decided to give out free money to attract deposits—say, $500 for each new $1,000—there would be riots in the streets, so eager would people be to get in on it.)

Even if your employer doesn't augment your own contribution, you should fund your 401(k) to the limit, because:

❖ It is a relatively painless way to save.

❖ You avoid taxes on the money you contribute until, many years later, you withdraw it.

❖ In the meantime, no tax is due as it grows.

You get "Uncle Sam's" share of your income working for you all those years as well as your own. The tax drag is lessened considerably.

And how to deploy the assets in your 401(k)? Well, this is long-term money, so you should choose the alternative that does best over the long term: stocks. There will be years when the value of your 401(k) drops sharply, because the stock market does that sometimes. But over the long run, the odds are in your favor. Unless you think you can outsmart the market (hint: you can't), the simplest and most sensible thing to do is just keep building your assets in the fund without trying to switch them in and out of the stock market.

If your plan offers an "international" stock market fund as well as a U.S. fund, you might split your money over both. We are by no means the only game in town anymore.

The most common mistake 401(k) participants make is to deploy their 401(k) assets too conservatively. Even as you near retirement, you shouldn't switch all your money out of stocks and into short-term or guaranteed safe stuff. *Some* of it, perhaps—especially if the stock market is high—but the thing to remember is that the onset of retirement is not the end of the game. A 60-year-old married, nonsmoking male in decent health has a life expectancy of 26 more years. And if he's a she, her life expectancy is 31 more years. So even though he or she is contemplating retirement, it's not as if all the 401(k) money will suddenly be withdrawn, spent on canes the first year, walkers the second, and bang—you're gone. With any luck, you still have the long term to provide for. And that means a good chunk of your money, as you near retirement, should stay in stocks. (Even after you leave your employer, there will be ways to roll your retirement money into other tax-deferred retirement accounts. If the market has taken a dive just before you retire, you could roll your stock-market retirement money into other stock-market funds and wait for it to recover.)

The second-most-common mistake 401(k) participants make—out of loyalty, often—is to bet too heavily on their own company's stock. You already have a lot riding on your company . . . your job, perhaps some stock options. To put all your retirement eggs in this one basket, too, is not prudent. Sometimes it will be smart—your company's stock may way outperform the market—but it will not be prudent. So unless you really know what you're doing, go easy on this alternative.

Note to 403(b) participants: Nonprofit organizations often offer a variant of the 401(k) called a 403(b) plan. Some of these offer investment choices that include only variable annuities and funds charging high expenses. A little-known loophole, however, allows the individual to have her contributions go to virtually any custodian that handles retirement accounts—mutual funds, for example—*if* the custodian is willing to establish a 403(b)-7 account. Before your eyes glaze over, let me assure you that you need only call the mutual fund you'd like to use, and ask them to help you with the details of having your existing funds and future contributions go to them. It is in their best interest to make it easy for you to switch your money to them. Your employer's benefit department may tell you this isn't possible, but unless the law changes, if you persist you will eventually convince them that they are wrong. The mutual fund trying to get your money will be your ally in providing proof that Congress permits this for all such plans. Don't overlook fees you may be charged for transferring existing retirement savings out of variable annuities or funds with back-end loads; but keep in mind that the custodians with the highest penalties are usually the worst investments, so the withdrawal penalty may hurt less in the long run than leaving the funds with them.

IRAs, Keogh Plans, and SEPs

If your employer doesn't offer a 401(k) or 403(b)—or even if he does—you can set up an IRA (Individual Retirement Account). If you're self-employed, you can set up a Keogh Plan or a SEP (Simplified Employee Pension).* You can do this at just about any bank, brokerage firm, or mutual fund. I recommend the mutual fund route because, again, this is your long-term retirement money. But the main thing is to *do* it, if you haven't already. Just pick up the phone and call one of the toll-free numbers on pages 222–25 ("Selected Mutual Funds"). They will send you the materials you need to start. Or walk down to your local bank and pick up the brochures that tell you how much you're allowed to con- tribute each year, how much of that will be deductible in your situation, how withdrawals are made, and all the rest.

Don't put money in these plans you might have to with- draw in a year or two, because you will suffer a 10% non- deductible penalty on any money withdrawn before age 59½ (*and* have to pay tax on the full withdrawal). But for

---

* You can also now establish a SIMPLE (Savings Incentive Match Plan for Employees), which is a form of 401(k) plan for small businesses. It requires virtually no paperwork or government filings—hence the acronym—and allows up to $6,000 in pre-tax dollars to be set aside in a special SIMPLE- IRA by each employee plus an employer match on contributions up to 3% of each employee's wages. Call your mutual fund family for details.

money you can set aside for the last 40% of your life (age 60 through 100), these are great places to put it.

Let's say you are 29½ and you contribute $2,000 to a Keogh Plan or IRA next week. At 10% it would compound to $34,899 by the time you were 59½ (when you can begin withdrawing it without penalty) and to $99,570 by age 70½ (when you *have to* start withdrawing it). Let's say you choose at that point to withdraw it all in a lump rather than extend the tax shelter by withdrawing just a little at a time. So at 70½ you'd withdraw $99,570, pay perhaps a third of it in taxes, and have $66,000 left.

Now look at that same $2,000 without the benefit of a Keogh Plan or IRA. If you had not contributed it to a Keogh Plan or IRA, aged 29½, the first thing that would have happened is that it would have been taxed. Again, say a third of it would have been lopped off in federal and local income taxes, leaving you with $1,333. If you had then invested that $1,333 at the same 10% a year, it would have grown—after paying a third in taxes—at just 6.7%. Thirty years later, aged 59½—assuming you had resisted the temptation to blow the money on lawn furniture—it would have grown to $9,243; by age 70½, to $18,798.

The first way, you are left with about $66,000; the second, $18,798. The Keogh Plan or IRA leaves you with more than three times as much money after tax, even though it requires absolutely no more to start with, no more risk or effort, and less self-discipline (because once it's locked up in the plan, you will not constantly be tempted to do something different with it).

And that's just $2,000, one year.

Which is good, because in 41 years $66,000 isn't going to buy nearly as much as it does today, and you golf maniacs are going to need a lot more than that to live comfortably within driving range of a driving range. *But no matter how much or little $66,000 buys 41 years from now, it will be a heck of a lot more than $18,798.*

The prime thing to note is the importance of starting early. Indeed, the contributions in your later years will add relatively little to the value of your fund. It is the early contributions which, compounded over time, grow enormously.

You could, for example, contribute just $1,000 a year from age 20 to 35 and then nothing. If you then withdrew the money between the ages of 65 and 80, your initial $15,000 would have grown (at 8%) to provide you well over $400,000!

If you assume your money will compound at 10% (as the U.S. stock market has, more or less, since 1926), then that initial $15,000 will provide you with more than $1 million. At 12% (as the market has if you start the clock after the Depression)—nearly $3 million. All from fifteen $1,000 contributions in your youth.

The problem, of course, is that the higher the rate of return you assume, the higher the rate of inflation you should assume, too. So $3 million may not buy all that much. But, as I say, it will buy a lot more than some lesser amount you would have set aside without the help of an IRA or Keogh.

So why doesn't everyone who qualifies for such a plan set one up and contribute to it to the maximum extent allowed? The primary objection comes from people who don't want to tie up their money so long.

Yet there are two very strong arguments against that objection. In the first place, you *can* withdraw money from these plans. Yes, you have to pay taxes and a penalty. But you would have had to pay taxes on that income, anyway, if you hadn't put it into the plan—so that part isn't so terrible. And the extra nondeductible 10%, while indeed stiff, may not be much to pay for having been allowed to compound your savings—as well as the portion the government would have taken—tax-deferred for several years.

Second and most important: Do you plan to have *any* money saved up by the time you are 59½? *Any* net worth? *Anything* to supplement your Social Security and the gen-

erosity of your children? If so—and for most people the answer is an emphatic *yes*—it may as well be in the form of a tax-free retirement fund. What can you lose by not paying taxes?

The Roth IRA

This is a good one. As long as your adjusted gross income is less than $95,000, you can contribute $2,000 a year to a Roth IRA. (If you file jointly with an AGI under $150,000, you can *each* have a Roth IRA and contribute $2,000.) This is permitted even if you are actively participating in other pension or profit-sharing arrangements.

Much has been made of the difficulty of deciding between the Roth IRA and the traditional IRA (since the $2,000 limit applies to the total placed in both), but it's really very simple: especially if you're young and/or in a low tax bracket, but even if you're not, you should probably open a Roth IRA and fund it to the maximum every year.

The basic difference between the Roth IRA and the traditional IRA, as you know, is that with the traditional one you get your tax break on the way in—your $2,000 contribution is deductible—whereas with the Roth IRA you get your break on the way out. Every penny you withdraw from the Roth IRA is tax-free. (Another advantage of the Roth IRA: you're not *required* to withdraw the money at all, let alone on a rigid IRS-dictated schedule. If you don't need it when you're 70½, you can let it keep growing until, say, you're 75 or 80, when you might.)

Theoretically, if your tax bracket will be the same at withdrawal as at the time of contribution, it makes no difference which you choose. To keep the math simple, say you're in the 50% bracket. One way, your full $2,000 grows for you, but gets chopped in half by taxes when you withdraw it. The other way, only $1,000 is left to invest after tax, but isn't chopped at all when withdrawn. (To keep it *really* simple, imagine that you only made this one contribution, in a mutual fund that tripled. So now you've got $6,000 in the traditional IRA and $3,000 in the Roth. You withdraw it, paying 50% tax on the $6,000, and look what's happened—you net $3,000 either way.)

So theoretically, you'd want to choose a Roth IRA if you're in a low bracket now and expect it might be higher when you retire; a traditional IRA if you're in a high bracket now and expect it to be lower when you retire.

But there's a flaw in all this theory. It assumes you'd put $2,000 in a traditional IRA or, after the tax bite, only $1,000 in the Roth. Hey! If you possibly can, put the full $2,000 in the Roth! That way, in the example above, you'd have $6,000—and be able to *keep* it.

In essence, a person who sets up a Roth IRA is saving more for the future. *And a person who saves more virtually always ends up with more.* The Roth IRA effectively tricks the taxpayer into saving more for retirement (because he has to come up with 2,000 real dollars, not 2,000 tax-deductible dollars)— and that's not a bad thing.

All of this discussion is moot for most people, anyway, since the deductible IRA is only available to people with relatively low incomes or no other active retirement plans. Since most workers have access to some form of retirement plan, they wouldn't be able to deduct their IRA contributions unless their income were low enough to place them in the lowest tax bracket—in which case they'd get little benefit from the traditional IRA in the first place!

It's always possible that Congress will do something sneaky that could negate the advantages of the IRA—like replace the income tax with a sales tax. There you'd be, having foregone a nice tax deduction year after year, all to avoid what turned out to be *no income tax after all!* Or perhaps one's Roth IRA withdrawals will be taken into consideration when deciding whether you actually "need" Social Security benefits. But that's unlikely, too. Do you know how many elderly voters there will *be* by the time your Roth IRA has a bunch of money in it? Do you know how testy they will get if Congress tries to enact backdoor taxation of the Roth IRA withdrawal?

There's also the issue of whether all 50 states will honor the spirit of the Roth IRA and exempt withdrawals from tax as Uncle Sam does. My guess is that they will.

So anything is possible, but to me the Roth IRA means more saving, more certainty (what you've saved is what you keep), and more flexibility at withdrawal.

(Not only need *you* not withdraw the money, your beneficiary can elect to stretch withdrawals over his or her life expectancy. A Roth IRA contribution at age 25 might compound tax-free for 60 years—and then for yet another 50 or 60 while your granddaughter, named as beneficiary, slowly removes the funds.)

The point is that the Roth IRA will usually be the best alternative, sometimes by a wide margin, while it will only occasionally be bested by the traditional IRA, and then usually by a small margin. Save yourself the trouble of agonizing over the choice, and go with the Roth IRA (unless your income is too high to qualify). Forget the worksheets.

A Few IRA/Keogh Fine Points

Naturally there are lots of details. Here are just a few:

❖ **What if I die or become disabled?** Upon death or permanent total disability—regardless of your age—the entire fund may be withdrawn without penalty, either all at once or over a period of years. If you die, the spouse named as beneficiary in your plan has the option of rolling over the proceeds of the fund into an IRA of his or her own. (Nonspousal beneficiaries can roll the proceeds into special "beneficiary IRAs," but must begin withdrawal at once.)

❖ **What if I have employees?** If you set up a Keogh Plan for yourself, you are required to make contributions for your employees, too. But you can set up the plan such that employees do not become eligible until they've been with you three years.

❖ **What if I'm *already* over 59½?** It's not too late to set up one of these retirement plans—and the tax savings can still be substantial.

❖ **What if I'm in a very low tax bracket now?** Then you should definitely choose a Roth IRA. Otherwise, you could be sheltering money from, say, a 15% tax rate today and shifting it into the future when you might be in the 40% rate (either because your fortunes improve and/or Congress raises the tax rates).

❖ **What about this awful 15% excise tax I've heard about?** It was pretty awful and applied to "excess distributions," in case you had saved too successfully. Happily, it's been repealed.

❖ **What's my deadline for setting up one of these and making contributions?** That's the wrong question. It assumes you want to wait till the last possible minute. In fact, you want to do it right away, if you can. Even if you just missed the "deadline" for this tax year, that just means you're getting the earliest possible start for next year. Interestingly, if you had two people each contributing $2,000 a year to an IRA for 25 years, earning 10%, but one contributed January 2 each tax year (the earliest possible moment) and the other waited until April 15 of the following year (the last possible moment), each would have contributed $50,000 in total over those 25 years. But the one who got the early start would have seen her money grow by an extra $20,000 or so, because it would have had longer to compound.

❖ **What about "nondeductible" retirement-plan contributions?** Many people have the opportunity to put "extra," nondeductible money into their employer's retirement plan, or to put money into an IRA even though they won't qualify for the tax deduction. When you do this, you shelter the growth of the money from taxes until withdrawn; and then only that growth is taxed when it *is* withdrawn. Not bad. But a Roth IRA is better, if you qualify. What's more, see the section on Stocks, at the end of this chapter.

❖ **What about early withdrawals?** Among the other advantages of a Roth IRA is the ability to withdraw contributions—not appreciation, but the money you actually contributed—free of tax or penalty at any time. This strikes me as a weak advantage at best, since the whole point is to keep as much money growing tax-free as you can. Though it's permitted, I'd think twice about withdrawing money from either a Roth or a traditional IRA for the down payment on a first home, or to pay catastrophic medical expenses or college costs. It's good to have this option, but it should be used as a last resort, since money withdrawn for these purposes cannot later be returned to the tax shelter. Better to borrow from your retirement plan at work, if possible—and then repay the loan as quickly as you can.

❖ **What about converting my existing IRA to a Roth?**It's as simple as filling out a little paperwork with the custodian of your current IRA, but can only be done in a year your adjusted gross income (not counting this conversion) will be under $100,000—big penalties if you screw up. (The penalty is avoided if—realizing your income will exceed $100,000—you reverse the conversion before April 15 of the following year.) You will have to pay tax on every penny you convert (except pennies that were contributed nondeductibly), but for someone with $17,397 saved up in an IRA, of which $12,000 represented six nondeductible $2,000 contributions, say, conversion is all but irresistible. He'd pay tax just on the $5,397 in appreciation, and from then on all growth would be tax-exempt forever. On the other hand, someone with $196,384 in her IRA, all subject to tax, would have to think twice. In the first place, this would put her in a high tax bracket if she were not already there. In the second, she wouldn't want to use some of the money *in* the IRA to pay the tax, because then she'd be reducing the size of her tax-sheltered fund.

So one possibility is to set up a Roth IRA and convert just a manageable portion of one's traditional IRA to it each year—particularly in years when, for whatever reason, your taxable income, and thus the tax you would pay, are low. Traditional IRAs are great. But where you can afford it, paying the tax to convert is like kicking in more money for your old age.

❖ **Further questions?** Write the nearest Internal Revenue Service office for IRS publication 590 and struggle through it, or ask the retirement expert at your bank, your employer, or your accountant to help you.

Kids and Retirement Plans

One last note to tie these two together—your kids (or grandkids) and retirement. Silly as it sounds at first, you might actually want to encourage your 12-year-old to set up a Roth IRA. Not because he will have the vaguest interest in saving for his retirement, but because the power of compound interest is so amazing (and, again, because of the saving habit it might help to form). Up to $2,000 a year in wages your child earns may be contributed to an IRA, so long as it's legitimate income, earned either from a family business (he stocks the shelves in your store) or from outside sources like baby-sitting or lawn-mowing (but not sitting *your* baby or mowing *your* lawn). It's also legal for you then to give your child enough to replace what he or she has squirreled away in the IRA.

Say your 12-year-old earns $20 a week—$1,000—which she puts in an IRA. Say, further, that you *give* her an extra $20 a week spending money to make up for what she puts away. That way, she won't mind.

What's the point? Well, if she does this for 10 years, through age 22 . . . and if she invests it in an IRA account with a mutual fund that manages to earn 10% a year . . . then at age 70 (don't laugh!) that $10,000 you helped her put away would be worth $1.5 million—enough to throw off $180,000 a year for 20 years, to age 90.

There's no magic to this (just the magic of *doing it*—how many readers of the previous paragraph do you think actually will?). And inflation will surely erode the value of that $180,000. But if we average 3% inflation over all those years, it would still be the equivalent of $25,000 or $30,000 a year for 20 years in today's buying power—not bad for ten annual contributions of $1,000. How many old folks do you know today who couldn't use a $25,000-a-year income boost? My dream (well, one of my dreams) is that long after you and I are gone, there will be comfortably retired 80-year-old guys playing poker saying, "Well, and so my Pappy read this little *book* when I was twelve, and . . . eh? . . . have I told you this one already?"

Don't worry about terrible inflation unraveling this strategy, either. If we have an inflationary tidal wave at some point, your child or grandchild would likely do fine. The buying power of *bonds* would get creamed by bad inflation, but equity mutual funds, with time, would likely bob up on top of the inflation. Why? Because they would own shares in the companies that are raising the prices! If hot dogs cost 20 times more than they do today, chances are that hot-dog makers' profits—of which they'd own a share—would eventually rise apace. And so would the value of their shares.

Annuities

Don't buy them! Annuities are hot these days because (a) they grow tax-deferred, and (b) they pay a fat commission to the folks who sell them—which leads to a lot of enthusiastic promotion.

Basically, annuities are like giant IRAs with no limit on how much you can contribute—but no tax deduction for making that contribution, either.

Some annuities promise a fixed return. Increasingly, people are buying *variable* annuities, where your return depends on how well the insurance company has invested your money. It's like investing your IRA in a stock-market mutual fund.

Since you're likely to hear a lot of reasons why you should buy annuities, here are a few why you should not:

1. Annuity income is fully taxed as you withdraw it. If you're looking for tax shelter, why not buy tax-free bonds instead? (See Chapter 5.) Their interest is *never* taxed.

2. The alluring rate some annuities promise is generally guaranteed for only one year. The computer printouts often used to sell them are typically illustrations of what *might* happen, not what's guaranteed.

3. Once you buy an annuity, your funds are pretty well locked in to age 59½. There's the 10% penalty, as with an IRA (but not the initial tax deduction that makes IRAs so attractive); and many annuities impose hefty surrender charges of their own.

4. Since annuities are typically bought for the *long term,* why not buy stocks instead? Over long periods of time, stocks are almost sure to beat fixed-rate investments.

5. Variable annuities do invest in stocks—but how well? What if the insurance company hires below-average managers? After all, not all money managers are above average. Or what if you want to switch to some other investment manager? At the very least, you would have to hassle with a "1035 Exchange," and you might face surrender charges as well.

6. Even if their investment managers are just as good as anybody else's, most variable annuities will significantly underperform because they are dragged down by heavy sales and overhead costs, and by an insurance component that does you little good.

7. In any event, if you're going to invest in stocks, *why do it through an annuity?* Yes, dividends will be shielded from tax until you withdraw them. But here's the flip side: *Any gains you withdraw from an annuity are fully taxed as ordinary income, even if they would have qualified as lightly taxed long-term capital gains outside the "shelter" of the annuity.* (This is true of traditional IRAs and Keogh Plans, too; but with those you get that very appealing initial tax deduction.) You are paying big fees to convert low-taxed capital gains into high-taxed ordinary income!

8. Appreciation within an annuity must eventually be distributed and subjected to income tax—when you die, if not before. Under current law, gains *outside* an annuity escape income tax altogether when you die. Good news for your loved ones.

In short: if you were thinking of a *fixed-rate annuity*, consider tax-free bonds instead. If you were thinking of a *variable annuity*, buy a no-load stock-market mutual fund instead. You'll save sales fees and insurance charges; you'll suffer no penalty for early withdrawal; you'll enjoy considerable, albeit different, tax advantages.

If you've already *bought* an annuity: good. It's great that you've put money aside and that it's growing tax-deferred. But with the next chunk of cash you're able to squirrel away, you might be able to do even better.

Two Exceptions:

❖ Teachers at tuition-based institutions have a pretty good deal with TIAA-CREF. If you're one of them, you know what I mean.

❖ If you're actually interested in buying an *annuity*—a real one—then go ahead. Long before annuities became highly promoted tax-deferral schemes for working folks, they were something almost entirely different—an insurance company's promise to pay you a set amount as long as you lived. For an 80-year-old not sure whether she will live another 3 years or another 30, it's a way to shift the "risk" of exceptionally long life onto an insurance company. The insurer can handle this risk because (a) it will assume, in setting its price, that you're likely to live a long time (terminal patients do not buy annuities); and (b) even if *you* live to 105, enough other annuitants won't, on average, the insurer makes out fine. Annuities are the opposite of life insurance, where insurers suspect all applicants of hereditary heart disease, and the customer "wins" by dying young. Just be sure, before you plunk down $300,000 for an annuity, that you've shopped aggressively for the best deal—and that you really want to do this. Once you've bought an annuity, there are no refunds.

Tax Shelters

Traditionally, the term "tax shelter" doesn't refer to an IRA or an annuity but rather to some scheme concocted by a promoter and a lawyer in the form of a limited partnership. You and a bunch of other wealthy individuals put in $25,000 or $250,000 each, taking a tax deduction, and suddenly you own your share of an apartment complex or an avocado orchard and get to spend the next 15 or 20 years complaining about how poorly it all worked out.

At best, tax shelters merely postpone taxes, they don't eliminate them. And tax shelters frequently go awry. Some are outright frauds; others are well-intentioned ventures that fail (as in the case of an oil well that comes up dry); and still others do not stand up to IRS scrutiny.

When the top marginal tax bracket is 90% (as it was pre-Kennedy) or 70% (as it was until 1980) or even 50% (until 1986), it is understandable that people will do almost anything to reduce the bite. But as tax brackets fall, the incentive to take insane risks and pay insane promotional fees and complicate one's tax return diminishes—or should.

Far better, countless investors have learned, to lose 40 or 50 cents of each dollar to the government than to lose the whole dollar.

Real Estate

Real estate you invest in on your own—where you know the area personally, search for your own opportunity and are intimately involved in structuring the deal and overseeing the property—is far different from the kind of tax shelter referred to above. The hand-tailored approach takes more effort but, done carefully, is less likely to go wrong.

The twist is that, for tax purposes, you get to depreciate your property, even as—in real life—it may be *app*reciating. Say you buy an eight-unit apartment building down the street in a bank foreclosure for $350,000, of which $275,000 is depreciable, and manage to clear $10,000 a year after all expenses. Because residential property is currently depreciated over 27.5 years, you get to deduct $10,000 a year in depreciation from your rental income— so in this example it's all tax-deferred until you sell. Meanwhile, say the property appreciates at 4% a year. That gain is shielded from taxes also until you sell. When you do sell, you have to pay capital gains tax not only on the 4% annual appreciation but also on all the accumulated depreciation. *But no one says you have to sell.* You could just keep collecting more and more rent—and perhaps one day borrow more against your now-more-valuable property to enjoy some of the gain without paying tax on it.

These are the basic tax advantages real estate offers. But real estate isn't an investment, it's a *business*. That's fine if you have the time, talent, and temperament. But it's sure a lot easier to pick up the phone and buy 1,000 shares of a company that invests in real estate (such as a "real estate investment trust" listed on the New York Stock Exchange) than to fix a tenant's toilet on a Sunday morning. Easier still to pick up the phone and *sell* those 1,000 shares than to sell your building.

Real estate, indeed, can be as much a part-time *job*— scouting for properties, arranging their purchase, fixing them up, interviewing tenants, keeping them happy, negotiating the bureaucratic maze, cajoling plumbers in emergencies—as an investment. Some people see only headaches and risks. Others see a chance to be creative, to build sizable equity (and even more sizable bank debt), and to run their own show. If you are one of the latter, there are a great many primers available, not to mention eager real estate brokers who may go so far as to offer to manage your properties for you for a percentage of the rent.

By all means buy that seaside motel as your semiretirement home and business. But recognize that that's what it is: a business . . . and that running a business is a job . . .

and that not all real estate *does* appreciate. Be sure you're getting a very good deal, and understand what you're getting into, before you buy.

Your Own Business

There are thousands of businesses besides real estate to go into. Among the potential tax advantages: the ability to set up larger-than-IRA retirement plans and to deduct the cost of your health insurance; the likely light taxation of any gain when you sell. And more. But it's a huge undertaking—and another book. This book is about your money, not about switching careers.

Your Own Home

You can't depreciate it. You don't even get any tax benefit if you wind up selling it at a loss, as you do with investments. But the higher your tax bracket, the more of the cost Uncle Sam shoulders by virtue of the tax deductions home ownership provides—mortgage interest and property tax. Meanwhile, paying off the mortgage provides a good method of "forced saving," as your equity builds month by month (albeit imperceptibly at first). Perhaps best of all, any gain when you sell your primary residence is tax-free up to $250,000 ($500,000 for a married couple) as long as you lived there for at least two of the previous five years before the sale. In fact, if you are renting out a single-family residence that has appreciated greatly, you might want to move into it for two years before selling, in order to convert the property into your primary residence and the price appreciation into tax-free income.

Stocks

Growing companies pay out little or nothing in the way of taxable dividends. Most of their profits are reinvested, and most of your return, it is hoped, will come in the form of long-term appreciation. The first advantage: tax on your gains is deferred until you actually choose to sell and take your profit. In the meantime, Uncle Sam's share of your capital is working for you alongside your own. The second advantage: long-term capital gains are taxed less heavily than ordinary income.

Charity

If you write large checks to charity each year, you can save a lot of money in taxes by giving appreciated securities instead. Not only do you get the tax deduction for the gift, you avoid the capital gains tax that otherwise would have been due. In the case of a stock you bought for $4,000 that's now worth $13,500, you could save as much as $2,660 (28% federal tax on the $9,500 gain), and possibly some local income tax as well, by giving the stock instead of cash. But be careful:

❖ Be certain to have your broker transfer the stock to the charity *before* she sells it and sends the charity the proceeds. If the stock is held in your name when it's sold, you pay the tax.

❖ Be certain you've held the shares (or the building, or the van Gogh) *at least a year and a day,* or the IRS will allow you to deduct only your original cost.

Of course, this doesn't make sense for small gifts. Apart from the hassle, the commission a charity would have to pay to sell $250 or $500 worth of Microsoft could easily eat up 10% or 15% of the gift. But if you're someone who likes to give $250 or $500 a year to several different charities, there's a solution. Open an account with the Fidelity Investments Charitable Gift Fund (800-682-4438). Transfer your $13,500 worth of stock to that account, for which you get an immediate charitable deduction, just as if you'd given it to the Red Cross. Then, from time to time, mail or fax instructions to Fidelity. They'll send out checks on your behalf as small as $250, investing the balance in the meantime in your choice of four different kinds of funds—so you may have even more to give away than you planned.

This is the poor man's way to set up a charitable foundation—the Ford Foundation, the Rockefeller Foundation, and now *Your* Foundation.

Fidelity's Gift Fund is also handy if you should get a windfall. Say you exercised the last of your Microsoft stock options this year and reaped $400,000, of which you'd like to give $100,000 to charity. The Charitable Gift Fund could be perfect. After all, there you are, a 32-year-old receptionist who just happened to be with Microsoft from the beginning. If you gave all $100,000 to your favorite charities this year, you'd be showered with love and appreciation—and *deluged* with requests next year. But what could you give next year? You're still a receptionist, albeit a darned good one, and you make $26,000 a year. But suddenly the people you gave $5,000 to last year are expecting $6,000 this year . . . and you were thinking more along the lines of $50, which for a guy or gal making $26,000 is a very nice gift. They'll hate you!

With $100,000 in the Gift Fund, you might decide to distribute $5,000 a year—out of the growth in the fund itself, with any luck, perhaps never dipping into the $100,000 at all. That way, you are perceived as a very generous person indeed—how many receptionists make $5,000 a year in donations?—and can enjoy and refine your giving over the years without undue stress.

Charitable Fine Points

❖ If you've given $250 or more to a charity, you'll need a receipt—not just your canceled check. Most charities send them automatically, since they are well aware of the regulation, but it's your responsibility to get them and keep them if you're ever audited. It's not good enough to get them a year or two later, when the audit notice comes. The receipts must be dated no later than the date you file the tax return claiming them as deductions.

❖ Receipts are supposed to make clear that you received nothing of significant value in return for your contribution, or else disclose the fair value of what you did receive—e.g., $40 of your $150 benefit ticket went for food and entertainment. You only get to deduct $110 even if you have witnesses who will swear you ate just *one dinner roll* the whole night and fell asleep three words into the after-dinner speech.

❖ If you give something other than cash, the charity is expected to provide only a description of the goods, not an estimate of their value. That's your job. Back when he was governor, President Clinton valued a pair of old shoes at $80. Your old shoes might not have the same cachet, and will almost surely be smaller, so you might value them at somewhat less.

❖ If you're giving something (other than marketable securities) valued above $5,000, an appraisal is usually required. Testimony from your aunt who knows antiques ("GAWgeous!") will not do it.

❖ If you go to a charity auction and buy a Warhol print, or the actual Bic used by Paul Simon to pen "Bridge over Troubled Water," you are entitled to deduct only that portion of your check, if any, that exceeds the fair market value of what you purchased. So if the estimate in the auction catalog is $1,500 and you snag it for $900, you get no charitable deduction. A lot of people take the full amount of the check as a deduction anyway, which is probably one of the reasons the IRS now requires receipts of the type mentioned above. Thirty years ago, my mother organized a very successful art auction in our barn. (I know you wouldn't expect this from a city boy like me, but we had a barn.) It raised a few thousand dollars for some worthy cause, and my father, knowing that most of the successful bidders were likely to write off 100% of their expenditures as charitable deductions, dubbed the event *Le Grande Tax Dodgerie.* I think he dubbed it in French so as not to corrupt "the children," much as we used to talk about feeding the D-O-G, so as not to excite "the dog." Of course, in our school, they started teaching French in the second grade. It was tax law that would come later.

❖ Just as it's rarely wise to invest in something brought to your attention by bulk mail, so is it risky to give money to a charity based on a slick or plaintive solicitation—let alone to a telemarketer calling on behalf of some charity over the phone (and keeping, often, 50% or more of your donation). One of the more remarkable examples was a group that granted the wishes of dying children. According to the *New York Times,* the group raised $237,000 in 1984. Of that, $10,000 went to grant wishes; the rest was spent on "professional fund-raising organizations, salaries, car rentals, jewelry, rent, unsecured personal loans, a VCR, and a videotape entitled *Sex Games.*" Call the Council of Better Business Bureaus (703-276-0100) for reports on specific charities, or send them $2 and a self-addressed envelope for a free copy of *Give but Give Wisely,* which rates charities across 22 parameters (4200 Wilson Blvd., #800, Arlington, VA 22203). Or write the National Charities Information Bureau for its free *Wise Giving Guide* (19 Union Square West, New York, NY 10003).

Charity and Your IRA

If you're planning to leave some money to charity when you die and you have an IRA, consider naming that charity as the beneficiary of your IRA. That will save the income tax your heirs would otherwise have to pay on it. Give your heirs "regular" money from outside your IRA instead— money on which income tax has *already* been paid. To the charity it won't make any difference (charities don't pay taxes), but to your heirs it will.*

Charity and Your Fortune

If you have a ton of dough and are planning to leave some of it to charity, there are tax advantages, once you're in your later years, to giving it while you're still alive. You give the cash (or the appreciated property) now, but arrange to receive all the income from it as long as you live. In the meantime, you get a tax deduction—now—for the "present value" of your gift. If you're 85, the present value is nearly as high as the gift itself, because the IRS doesn't realize you're one of those feisty old codgers who's gonna be playing tennis for another 20 years. If you're 50, there's no point bothering with this, because the present value of your gift will be very small. But you might want to mention it to your folks. Almost any large charity will eagerly walk you through the basics of this. And then you might want to discuss it with your accountant and the attorney who prepared your will.

Tax Books and Software

Whatever the shape of the tax code by the time you read this, there will almost surely be a current edition of J. K. Lasser's *Your Income Tax* to guide you through it. It's filled with examples and clear explanations. Just look in the index for what you need. *Consumer Reports* and H&R Block have good books, too.

If you have a computer, buy the current *TaxCut* or *TurboTax* and use them to prepare your taxes. It's cheap

---

* One small drawback: with a charity as the beneficiary, you might be required by IRS regulations to withdraw money from the IRA faster, once you turn 70½, than if, say, your spouse were the beneficiary, thus exposing more of it to taxation.

and easy, and you can always go to your accountant the first time to have him check over what you've done. Or, if your tax situation is complex, let the accountant keep doing your taxes, but use these programs to check his work. I once found a $2,000 error my mom's excellent accountant made in the IRS's favor. Nobody's perfect.

PART two

The Stock Market

The problem with trying to beat the market is that professional investors are so talented, so numerous, and so dedicated to their work that as a group they make it very difficult for any one of their number to do significantly better than the others, particularly in the long run. . . . [It is] so easy, while trying to do better, to do worse.

—CHARLES D. ELLIS,
Investment Policy: How to Win the Loser's Game

CHAPTER 7

Meanwhile, Down at the Track

October. This is one of the particularly dangerous months to speculate in stocks. Others are November, December, January, February, March, April, May, June, July, August, and September.

—MARK TWAIN

OK. You have some money in a savings bank; you are contributing to your company's 401(k) at the maximum rate allowed; you have equity in a home, if you want it; you've tied up $1,000 in bulk purchases of tuna fish and shaving cream; you have lowered your auto and homeowner's insurance premiums by increasing your deductibles; you have adequate term life insurance; you've paid off all your 18% installment loans and insulated your attic—you have done, in short, all the things that scream to be done.

Now what?

There are three compelling reasons to invest a large portion of your remaining funds in stocks:

1. **Over the long run—and it may be a very long run—stocks will outperform "safer" investments.** The reason is that stock and bond prices are set in the open market—and the market, over the long run, rewards risk. From 1926 to mid-1998, according to Ibbotson Associates, who track these sorts of things, the total compounded annual rate of return you would have had from buying risk-free United States Treasury bills was 3.8%; the return from slightly riskier corporate bonds would have been 5.7%; the return from blue-chip stocks

would have been 11%; and the return from the stocks of small companies would have been 12.7%.* The compounded annual rate of inflation during the same period was 3.1%. Ignoring taxes, $1,000 invested in Treasury bills over that time span would have grown to $14,250— but to $55,400 in corporate bonds, $1,828,000 in large stocks, and $5,520,000 in small stocks.

Of course, you can play with numbers like these, depending on the time periods you choose. There were some pretty dreadful five- and ten-year stretches nestled in among those 72 years (in case you hadn't noticed), during which you would have been much better off in bonds or even a savings account.

There was, for example, the period from September 1929 to June 1932, during which the U.S. stock market dropped 83%. Smaller stocks fared even worse, losing 92% of their value. If that seems like ancient history, large stocks lost 43% between January 1973 and September 1974, and small stocks were clobbered by more than 70% in the six years from late 1968 to late 1974— the first six years of my own investing career, which has made me rather cautious ever since.

But time heals all wounds. When the New York Stock Exchange celebrated its 200th birthday in May 1992, it could report that a person who bought shares in all of the companies on the exchange on *any* day in

---

* Stock returns include dividends. When you read that the market historically averages a gain of 9% or 10% a year, that's 6% or 7% appreciation, on average, and 3% or 4% from dividends. Lately, average dividends have been very low—under 2%. This is partly because stock prices have risen so high (a $1 dividend on a $20 stock is 5%, but falls to 1% as the stock rises to $100) and partly because CEOs have taken to using profits to buy back shares of the company stock rather than pay dividends. They will tell you this is because stock gains are taxed lighter than dividends, so their shareholders would prefer to see the stock rise (as it likely will if the company keeps buying it) than receive a fully taxable dividend check. What they won't tell you is that the bulk of their own compensation comes from stock options—so they have little interest in paying out cash that could be used to boost the stock price.

its history would have made a profit over *any* 15-year stretch and would have beaten bonds and savings accounts over any period exceeding 20 years.

Wharton finance professor Jeremy Siegel actually managed to come up with data for stock and bond performance stretching all the way back to 1802. A single dollar invested in stocks would have grown to $955,000 or so by 1990, he concluded—not quite 8% a year compounded. After taxes and inflation: a "mere" $43,100. The same dollar invested in safer long-term government bonds, after taxes and inflation, would have been worth $213.

Will the American economy be as dynamic over the *next* couple of centuries? I happen to think so, even if the next year or three in the stock market should prove disappointing. So now the only problems are (a) to be sure to set aside that dollar; and (b) somehow to remain spry enough to enjoy it.

When this book was revised in 1983, things had recently been dismal. Inflation nearing 20%, unemployment topping 10%, and the widespread conviction that every car on the road would soon be made in Japan. Yet it seemed then that "it just might be that we have been going through a toughening-up process over the last several years, and that our sensational technological prowess has been paving the way for enormous strides forward."

The stock market quadrupled in the 12 years that followed.

And for the future? Here's what I wrote in 1995, at the last revision:

Technology races ahead faster than ever, a tremendous force for productivity and prosperity. And where for decades the defense budget siphoned off around 6% of our gross domestic output (compared with 1% for the Japanese—a huge competitive disadvantage), today that largely nonproductive spending has dropped to more like 3.5%. At the same time, there's been a sweeping worldwide movement toward free trade and capitalism. Considering these broad forces, the heights to which the U.S. stock market had risen by 1995, while scary, were not totally unfounded. It was not, by and large, a "bubble." Specific stocks may collapse (I can think of a few candidates), but the overall market, no matter where it goes from here, will, over the long run, go much higher.

All that remains true (and defense spending is now under 3% of our Gross Domestic Product). Stocks have *soared* since 1995, leaving me all the more nervous for the short run. But the future holds great promise. The eternal question when times are good and hopes bright: how much of that promise is already reflected in stock prices? And what if things go wrong?

"If you're looking out 40 years," famed investor John Templeton told *Mutual Funds* magazine in early 1995, "I think you can probably do 15% a year. [The short-term outlook is not as rosy, he said, because we're coming off such a rapid run-up already.] A strong reason is that progress is speeding up. The improvements in most companies and industries are coming faster and faster. It's been an absolutely marvelous time to live. Just in my [82-year] lifetime, the world standard of living has quadrupled, and that's amazing. Through history, it took 1,000 years to double the standard of living. The reasons why it is speeding up have not stopped; in fact *they've* speeded up. Take the amount of money spent on scientific research. Eighty-two years ago, the world spent about $1 billion every three months. Now the world is spending $2 billion a day."

When the next real bear market comes, it's likely to be a killer, because so few investors or money managers today have ever really lived through one. But guess what. If you hang in there, and invest more as the fainter-hearted panic and prices grind steadily lower month after excruciating month, in the long run you'll do just fine.

2. **Unlike bonds, stocks offer at least the potential of keeping up with inflation,** even if that potential is by no means always realized. Once the interest rate on a bond is set, it's set. Bread could go to $20 a loaf, and the bond wouldn't pay a nickel more in interest. But the company that bakes the bread might—*might*—be able to keep its profits, and its dividend, rising in step with inflation.

3. **If all goes well, stocks can act as a tax shelter.** Long-term capital gains are generally taxed less heavily than ordinary income. And *no* tax is due on your gains until you choose to take them. Only the dividends face immediate taxation.

   Because many companies pay out relatively little of their profits in dividends, you pay relatively little tax on your share of those profits. Instead, the company retains and reinvests them for you. If they do a good job, future profits, and your share of them, will be even larger. This is the bird-in-the-bush strategy of investing. With it, you can ultimately profit two ways. First, after a period of years the company may decide to pay out a greater portion of its (by-then-fatter) profits as dividends. Second, you can sell your stock. If the company has invested your profits wisely, there is a reasonable chance you will get more for it than you paid—perhaps even several times as much.

   It thus becomes a matter of some interest just how well a company is likely to reinvest all those profits they don't pay you as dividends. Unfortunately, there is no way to know for sure. However, you can determine how well they've done—or, because accounting is open to so much qualification and interpretation, how well they seem to have done—in the past. The number you are looking for is "return on equity," and it is, simply, the company's profits expressed as a percentage of all the money shareholders have dumped in over the years, much of it by forgoing dividends.

There are companies that have been able to reinvest those accumulated unpaid dividends at returns well above 15% a year. Others have earned less than half as much. And then there are those that have diddled it away altogether. (Does the name Eastern Airlines ring a bell? Pan Am? Braniff? People's Express? Have I mentioned Marvel Toys?)

Investors would naturally prefer stock in companies more like the former than the latter, all other things being equal. So all other things are *not* equal. You have to pay more for stock in companies that are known to reinvest profits at a high rate of return. Indeed, there was a time (1973) when you had to pay $60 or more to get a $1 slice of Avon's profit pie, so excited were investors by Avon's ability to earn 25% on that dollar.* At the same time it cost only $8 to buy a $1 slice of Goodrich's slower-growing profit pie. What investors failed to note was that, although 25% was a boffo return on that one reinvested Avon dollar, a dollar—no matter how well it was reinvested—was a pretty lousy return on a $60 investment! Subsequently Avon stock fell about 85% even though profits kept growing. And then, after a few years, profits started shrinking. By 1997, earnings had climbed back smartly and the shares had finally climbed back to their 1973 peak. But 24 years is a long time to wait.

So there's more to choosing the right stock than finding the company with the highest "return on equity." But I'm getting ahead of myself. I should not talk like this until you know as much about the essentials of the stock market—the forest—as the professionals do. This

---

* Avon was earning a little over $2 in profit for each of its shares. The shares went for $70 apiece (adjusted for a subsequent split).

will take up most of the rest of the chapter. (Getting to know as much about the trees could take up most of the rest of your life.)

The stock market could hardly be simpler. There are just two ways a stock can go: up or down. There are just two emotions that tug in those opposite directions: greed and fear. There are just two ways to make money on a stock: dividends and capital gains. And there are just two kinds of investors in the market: the "public," like you or me; and the "institutions," like mutual funds and pension funds. It's the amateurs against the professionals, and it's not all that clear who has the advantage. Often, both lose.

The bottom line, if you want to cut straight to the chase, is that most people should do their stock-market investing through no-load index mutual funds. If you do, you will outperform at least two-thirds of all your friends and neighbors—including many who work much harder at this than you. But if you do decide to go it alone, either because you believe you can beat the pros or because it's fun to try, read on.

What is a stock worth? Market veterans will tell you that a stock is worth whatever people are willing to pay for it. Price is determined by supply and demand. If lots of people want it, it will be worth a lot. If everyone ignores it, it won't be worth spitting at.

But it is too simple to say that a stock is worth whatever people will pay for it, because what people are willing to pay for it depends on what they think it is worth. It is a circular definition, used as a rationalization of financial foolishness rather than as a rational way to appraise value.

The value of a stock should not be nearly so subjective as, say, the value of a Picasso sketch or an Einstein-penned letter. A share of stock merely entitles the owner to a share of present and future profits (or, in the event of bankruptcy or acquisition by another company, assets). Where two paintings of equal size may reasonably command vastly different values, two companies of equal profits, assets, and prospects should not. Yet do.

The market veteran will readily agree that this is irrational, but he will ask you, with a laugh, "Who ever said the stock market was rational?"

That gets the market veteran off the hook and may eliminate in his mind the need to search for value. But there are other market veterans, perhaps even a majority by now, who believe that rationality does pay off in the market over the long run. Sooner or later, they say, bubbles burst; sooner or later, bargains are recognized. A company cannot prosper forever without its shareholders at some point benefiting.

Indeed, if the market is driven by irrational greed and fear to excesses of over- and undervaluation, as it surely is, then it is the rational man, they say, seeing these excesses for what they are, who will be buying the excessively undervalued stock, particularly when the market as a whole is depressed; and selling the excessively overvalued stock, particularly when the market as a whole is flying high. Thus may he profit from the swings in between.

All of this assumes that a rational man can determine what a stock is "really" worth.

Rational men differ. A company's future prospects—and even its current profits—are open to widely differing assessments. Obviously, no one can answer precisely what a stock is worth. But that doesn't eliminate the need to arrive at some rational valuation, or the possibility of setting some reasonable guidelines for doing so.

What a stock is worth depends at any given time on the alternative investments that are then available. It is a question of relative value. Think of investments as wallets. A 5% savings account is a wallet you can buy for $20 that miraculously fills up with $1 (5%) by the end of every year. It is safe and convenient—you can "sell" it whenever you want and be sure of getting back your full $20—but it's not a great investment. At the time of this writing you can buy other "wallets" that fill up with the same $1 just as fast—

not for $20 but for a mere $15. Namely, high-grade corporate bonds that pay 6.7% interest.

You can say that the first wallet sells for "20 times earnings" and the second for "15 times earnings." This is the famous "price/earnings ratio," or "multiple," you have heard so much about, although it's generally applied to stocks, not bonds or wallets.*

Now, if a nearly risk-free investment like a high-grade bond sells for 15 times earnings, what should a stock sell for?

On the one hand, a stock should sell for *less*, because it involves more risk. There is no guarantee that the $1 will show up in the wallet by the end of the year—or even that the wallet itself will be in any shape to be sold to someone else, should you so desire. What's more, only a portion of your $1 is actually paid out to you as a cash dividend. Much, most, or all of it may be retained by the company. So, really, stocks should sell for way under 15 times earnings.

On the other hand, a stock should perhaps sell for *more*, because of its greater potential for gain (the earnings and/ or stock price could go up) and because of the tax advantages referred to earlier. So, really, stocks should sell for way *over* 15 times earnings.

In deciding how much more or less to pay for a stock than the 15 times earnings you might pay for a high-grade bond—or whatever the going rate is at the time you read this—one weighs the extra risk against the potential for extra return.†

---

* You will find "p/e ratios" listed, along with dividends and prices, in the stock pages of most newspapers.

† Up until 1958, stocks consistently yielded more in dividends than bonds yielded in interest. And "for a simple reason," writes Morgan Stanley's Byron Wien: "Stocks were known to be riskier than bonds, and therefore should provide a higher current reward." For that to be true again today, the Dow Jones industrial average would have to fall back from around 9000 to around 2100. (At which point people would surely perceive stocks as risky, and demand a high current reward for owning them.)

For a stock in a dull company whose earnings over the long run seem about as likely to increase as to fall—where risk and reward about cancel one another out—you might expect to pay 15 times earnings. So if you find such a stock selling for 8 or 10 times earnings, it could look pretty good.

For stock in a company whose earnings seem likely to be able to keep pace with inflation—no "real" growth, that is, but growth in earnings all the same—you might expect to pay more than the 15 times earnings you would pay for a high-grade bond, the earnings of which do not rise with inflation. In fact, some such companies sold at 5 or 6 times earnings back in 1974 and 1982. A bargain? You bet.

Finally, for stock in a company whose prospects are really bright, with the possibility of real growth of 5% or 10% or even 20% a year for the foreseeable future, you might expect to pay a lot more than 15 times earnings.

All other things being equal—that is, if all stocks were selling at 15 times earnings—you would choose only those companies whose earnings were expected to grow the fastest. But the question is not whether a fast-growing company is better than a slow-growing one. Any fool knows that. The question is whether you should pay 35 times earnings for the one or 12 times earnings for the other. Which stock, at any given time, is a better relative value? The real trick—and payoff—is to find a company selling for 12 times earnings that you think will grow as fast as the one selling for 35 times earnings. Then you know for sure which to buy.

Admittedly, it's not quite this simple. For one thing, it makes sense to look not just at what a company may earn but also at what it owns. A company whose business is lousy, but which happens to be conducted on 50,000 acres of wholly owned real estate between Dallas and Fort Worth, might have a liquidation value—if you closed down the business and paid off all the creditors—of $25 a share. Yet such land, if it had been acquired earlier in the century, might be valued on the company's books at next to nothing—so it might not even show up in quick calculations of the company's "book value." It could be what's known as a hidden asset, and well worth buying shares in, regardless of the company's dismal earnings.

I should also stress that the 15 times earnings I've been using as a benchmark is by no means eternal. It all depends on what wallets are going for at any given time. If you can get 15% from a high-grade bond, as you could in 1982, then you have a low-risk wallet that produces $1 for every $6.67 you put up—6.7 times earnings. The higher the prevailing long-term interest rate, the less you should be willing to pay for stocks. And vice versa. That old seesaw again.

Now it happens that far from looking at assets or relative value, the professional money managers of the late sixties and early seventies, when I was getting my first exposure to all this, concentrated their attention and their megabucks on a relative handful of fast-growing companies, bidding their prices up to truly remarkable heights. The "nifty fifty," these stocks were called—"glamour" stocks, "one-decision" stocks (you just had to decide to buy them; you would never sell them, no matter what price you could get). The group included such indisputably fine companies as Polaroid, Disney, Avon, Merrill Lynch, Xerox, and Coca-Cola.

Barron's' first issue of 1973 bore this headline: "Not a Bear Among Them. Our Panel Is Bullish on Wall Street." Uh-oh. When everyone is bullish—meaning, they think the market will rise—watch out: they've done their buying, and now are waiting for others to bid the stocks up even higher. But the "others" have already done *their* buying, too. There's no one left to buy! It's vaguely like your basic cartoon where the rabbit races out past the edge of a cliff, looks backward and forward to see where everybody is, and then plunges. Only with bulls, not rabbits.

Here's how some of the best-known stocks of that period fared, from their highs of 1972 to their lows of 1974:

What a Real Bear Market Looks Like

	1972	1974	Change
Avon	$140.00	$ 18.62	−87%
Coca-Cola	149.75	44.63	−70
IBM	341.38	150.50	−56
Intel	56.00	10.25	−82
Johnson & Johnson	133.00	73.13	−45
Kodak	151.75	57.63	−62
McDonald's	77.38	21.25	−73
Merrill Lynch	46.00	6.25	−86
Polaroid	149.50	14.13	−91
Procter & Gamble	112.75	67.00	−41
Walt Disney	211.63	30.75	−86
Xerox	171.88	49.00	−71

Prices unadjusted for subsequent stock splits

Most stocks the pros ignored altogether. Not because they lacked merit, although some did, but because it's a lot less trouble to put $100 million into Johnson & Johnson than to stay late at the office each night hunting for 50 less-visible companies—perhaps better values—in which to invest $2 million each. The first rule of fiduciary bureaucracy was (and is): You can't be criticized for losing money in IBM. Corollary: He who does what everyone else does will not do appreciably worse. In other words, it was *unfortunate* to lose money in IBM, Avon, Polaroid, or Xerox; but it would have been *imprudent* to lose (somewhat less) money in stocks no one ever heard of.

In talking with people who managed billions of pension-fund dollars at some of the nation's largest banks during this period, I got the distinct impression that it would have been *undignified* for top-drawer financial institutions like theirs to invest in anything but large, top-drawer American corporations.

That posture has a fiduciary ring to it, until you consider how much extra they were paying to invest in such firms, and how much they ultimately lost for their clients by doing so.

One major money manager told me that it was his bank's policy to invest only in companies whose earnings they expected to grow at an above-average rate. What about companies they expected to grow at only an average or subaverage rate? No, he said, they did not buy stock in such companies. Regardless of price? Regardless of price. Was there any price at which the bank would buy stock in an average company?

This question made the money manager uncomfortable. He clearly wanted to answer no, because he clearly would be damned before he would buy stock in such a company. But he couldn't come right out and say that, because he knew that, theoretically, there must be *some* price at which he should choose the stock of the mediocre company over the stocks of his nifty fifty.

On Wall Street, this sort of irrationality happens all the time. It's not impossible to profit from it, if you have an eye for value, nerves of steel, and a level head—but only with hindsight is it easy.

Subject to the caveats and additional suggestions in the next chapters, here's the most sensible way for most people to invest in stocks:

1. **Only invest money you won't have to touch for many years.** If you don't have money like that, don't buy stocks. People who buy stocks when they get bonuses and sell them when the roof starts to leak are entrusting their investment decisions to their roofs.

2. **Buy low and sell high.** You laugh. Yet most people, particularly small investors, shun the market when it's getting drubbed and venture back only after it has recovered and appears, once again, to be "healthy." It is precisely when the market looks worst that the

opportunities are best; precisely when things are good again that the opportunities are slimmest and the risks greatest.

Item: At what was probably the most opportune time to buy stocks since the Great Depression, December of 1974, with the Dow Jones industrial average struggling to break above 600 and countless lesser stocks selling for a half or a third or even a quarter of their book values, financial columnist Eliot Janeway was advising small investors to stay away. "No investment market in the coming year," he said with his customary self-assurance, "is going to be safe for civilians." In point of fact, the Dow climbed 40% in 1975, and many of the stocks that had been battered far worse than the Dow "blue chips" doubled and tripled.

Item: A Washington, D.C., investment club purchased 200 shares of a stock at 18. "Club sold all holdings at 12½," it reported to *Black Enterprise* magazine, "*due to decline in price;* intends to reinvest *when price moves up.*" (Italics mine.) What kind of strategy is *that?*

Torn as we all are between greed and fear, we tend to do just the wrong thing. When the economy is sinking fast and stocks faster, we get more and more scared. Finally, we quit in disgust. Better to get out with the big loss, we say to ourselves, than to watch our holdings disappear altogether. In fact, of course, this is just the time to be getting into the market, not out.

By the same token, avoid getting carried away with enthusiasm when the market is generally judged to be healthy, when you are becoming excited by the gains in some of the stocks you already own, when prospects for the economy are generally conceded to be bright, and when people are talking about the real possibility that the Dow Jones industrial average will finally break through to new ground. In such a climate people are expecting good news. If it comes, it won't move the market much because it has been so widely anticipated. If, by chance, bad news should come instead, that *will* move the market—down.

Whether concerning an individual stock, or the market as a whole, always ask yourself which would be more of a surprise: good news or bad news. News that is expected never has as much impact—if any at all—as news that is not.

"The truth is," market analyst Dr. Martin Zweig has written,

that the stock market does its best when earnings and dividends are getting drubbed, and worst when [they] are zooming. For example: In the fourth quarter of 1972 and the first quarter of 1973 . . . earnings of the Dow Industrials soared upward by 35% over year-earlier periods. The market responded by crashing more violently than at any time since the thirties. Then, amid the depths of pessimism, first- and second-quarter 1975 Dow profits collapsed an average of 31%; yet the stock market simultaneously vaulted 43%, one of the best six-month surges in history.

Another of the very best six-month surges was the explosion that began in August 1982. Unemployment was higher than at any time since the Depression, business leaders had finally lost confidence, the international banks were widely believed to be all but officially bankrupt, the federal deficit was exploding—and the market soared.

It works the same way, only in reverse, when the market is peaking.

"One reason that so many investors get overloaded with stocks at market tops," Zweig continues,

is their ill-founded reasoning: "Business looks good." It always looks good at the peaks. With prospects ripe for continued gains in earnings and dividends, investors optimistically lick their chops in anticipation of further market appreciation. But something goes astray. Business gets too overheated; the scramble for borrowed money to keep the boom rolling grows more intense, pressuring interest rates upward. The Federal Reserve, spotting increasing inflation, begins to tighten monetary growth, further exacerbating the surge in interest rates. Then, as short-term money instruments such as Treasury bills become more yield-attractive, the stock market begins to groan as the switching away from stocks accelerates, aided in no small part by the illiquidity in overly optimistic investors' portfolios [investors, that is, who have spent all their money on stocks already, and now have no more cash with which to buy any more]. Yet, most folks just continue holding their stocks—or worse, buying more—because "Business looks good." Finally, many months later it becomes apparent that business has slowed down . . . but it's too late for most investors. They've already been trapped by a crumbling stock market. "Optimism" gives way to "hope" that the business slowdown won't become a recession. But the drop in stock prices rocks consumer confidence, business dips some more and recession is reality. The stock market slump becomes a rout and investors' "hopes" are finally dashed. Seeing that a recession is in progress, investors "know" that earnings will slump; in "panic" they sell their stock, absorbing huge losses. Finally, all that selling, amid tons of pessimism, improves stock market liquidity [people once again have some cash], building a base for a new boom in the market . . . one which *always* begins before business turns up.*

That's the cycle, all right, but it's a lot easier to identify in hindsight than on any given Tuesday afternoon. If in the early sixties you had held off investing while you waited for the next recession, you would have had to sit on the sidelines for six or eight years. "Business looked good"—and was good—for nearly a decade.

Similarly, if you had gotten into the market after its 508-point October 19, 1987, crash, you would have

---

* The Zweig Forecast, Box 360, Bellmore, NY 11710.

done great . . . but had you gotten out when profits were soaring a few years later and the market had left its old highs in the dust, you would have missed a spectacular gain.

So for most people, the most practical, prudent way to avoid buying at market tops and selling at bottoms is to:

3. **Diversify over time by not investing all at once.** Spread your investments out to smooth the peaks and valleys of the market. A lifetime of periodic investments—adding to your investment fund $100 a month or $750 a month or whatever you can comfortably afford—is *the* ticket to financial security.

Steady periodic investing also gives you the benefits of *dollar-cost averaging*. Part of the theory here is that if you are in a terrible rush to buy the 300 shares, convinced the stock is about to take off and there's not a minute to lose, you are very likely reacting to some hot news. And believe me, unless you are trading (illegally) on inside information, chances are you are one of the last to hear this hot news. Nine times out of ten you will be buying your shares from someone who heard it first. In which case, when the dust settles you may not regret having snagged only 100 shares instead of 300. If, on the other hand, you are not reacting to any particular news when you decide to purchase the stock, it is simply unlikely that the stock would go straight up without any dips from the day you buy it. And dips allow you to average down your cost.

Attracted by its 9% yield and hopelessly ignorant of its problems, I once bought 50 shares of Con Edison, New York City's power company—Rock of Gibraltar—at 20. Shortly thereafter, Con Ed omitted its quarterly dividend for the first time in twelve thousand years and, to my dismay, I found myself buying 100 more shares at 12. Then 100 more at 8½. Then, even, 100 more at 6. I kept buying because I just could not believe that the State of New York—which needed only to grant Con Ed's rate requests to solve all its problems—would prefer to have the company go bankrupt, and thus have to take on the burden of power generation itself. (Especially considering New York's own financial position at the time.) Sure enough, the state began cooperating, the dividend gradually was restored (even raised a notch), and the stock recovered to 20. (It would later go on to double and split.) I would be lying if I told you I was smart enough to hold all 350 shares, or even most of them, all the way back up to 20 and beyond. But at least I held some. And I made sure that the first 50 shares I sold were the 50 I had purchased at 20, thus giving me a nice loss to help out with my taxes. The last shares I sold I had held long enough to qualify for long-term capital gain.

Strictly speaking, dollar-cost averaging is a little fancier than what I've described here. Strictly speaking, the idea is to invest in a stock, or in the market, in equal dollar amounts on a regular basis—say, $3,000 mailed to a mutual fund faithfully at the end of each year. By doing so, you will buy more shares when the fund is low and fewer when it is high. And look what happens. Say the price of shares in the Sakoff Illustration Fund (and hence the number you can buy) fluctuates as follows: $25 (so your first $3,000 buys 120 shares), $45 (so your next $3,000 buys only 67 shares), $25 (120 shares again), $5 (600 shares), $25 (120). The shares went up $20, came back, went down $20, and came back again. (This is, remember, the Sakoff Illustration Fund.) Yet even though the shares are no higher than when you started—$25—and even though they went down as much as they went up and averaged $25, do you think you wind up with only the $15,000 you put in? No, you wind up with—*ta-da!*—$25,675. That's dollar-cost averaging. It forces you to buy more shares when they're low, fewer when they're high.

The problem with what I did with Con Ed and what you just did so nicely with the Sakoff Illustration Fund is that *some stocks don't recover*. Con Ed made it, but many don't. You can lose a fortune buying more and more as a stock gets cheaper and cheaper. Trust me—I know. The stock *market,* on the other hand, "always" recovers.* And so will most broad-based stock-market mutual funds.

In truth, your fondest wish should be for a long and devastating bear market to begin right after you start your periodic investments. If you are a systematic investor, you should welcome declines with open arms and a checkbook. At the end of the day, when the market recovers, you'll be sitting pretty.

Diverting a portion of your paycheck to the market each month is a discipline that actually makes it easier to handle market declines, because you can focus on the bargain prices you are getting for your newly invested money rather than the shrinkage of your fortune. But until you've been through a major bear market in stocks, you won't know for sure that you have the emotional stability to stay with your investments when they suffer a substantial, prolonged decline in price, as one day they surely will.

4. **And then—for the most part—just stick with it.** As your periodic investments mount, hold on.

Sure, it could make sense to sell a few shares if you come to think the market is hugely overvalued and you just happen to be looking for $20,000 to back a friend's new software start-up (kiss *that* cash good-bye) or $50,000 to build an addition to your house.

Sure, it could make sense (because of taxes) to keep your *regular* money fully invested but shift some of your *tax-sheltered* retirement money out of stocks and into a money-market fund for a year or two, until the values appear more reasonable.

---

* Barring a 1917-style Soviet revolution or that kind of thing.

Sure, it could make sense to take money out of stocks and shift it into something that's gone through a terrible bear market of its own—as farmland did in the mid-eighties, while stocks were zooming, or as junk bonds did when the government forced banks to sell them.

But by and large, for your long-term money, "buy and hold" is the way to go.

Had you bought all the stocks in the table on page 130 and just stuck with them as they dove lower and lower from their all-time highs in 1972 and 1973, an original investment of $12,000—$1,000 in each stock—would now be worth around $300,000. (Then again, had you somehow had the brilliance to invest that $12,000 at the bottom instead of the top, it would now be worth three times as much.) Even if you had bought the four worst performers on the list—Avon, IBM, Polaroid, and Xerox—you'd now have twice as much money as if you'd kept the money in a savings account. But if you needed the money in just 20 years, say, instead of 25, you would have shown a hefty loss.

Part of the problem is knowing when the market is wildly overvalued. With hindsight, it was obvious in 1929 and 1987—and in Japan in 1990 (when the Nikkei index was 40,000; eight years later it was 16,000). But at the time? Well, if you read *Forbes* or *Barron's* you may get some clue. But there's a risk in that, too. You'll get interested! You'll start playing the market! You'll forget that you're just trying to spot those thrice-in-a-lifetime bubbles and start trying to spot subtler over- and undervaluations instead.

And there's this problem: It's not as if the Nikkei—wildly overvalued at 40,000 yen—was not also wildly overvalued at 25,000 yen. It was! Yet imagine you, the young Japanese with his or her money in the market, bailing out at 25,000 and watching all your friends reap it month after month as the market steadily climbed and climbed and climbed and . . . at some point you might have jumped back in, having missed much of the gain but fully exposed to the upcoming loss.

Worse, imagine that you had held on as it climbed to 40,000 and *still* held on. You had read the Japanese version of this same "buy and hold" advice. And for a couple of years—which is a long, depressing length of time when you are losing money every day—you watch your portfolio fall. And then for three years you watch it sit at about 40% of its former glory. And *still* Japanese stocks are, by some measures, badly overvalued, with the chance prices could be cut in half yet again! So do you sell then? Or *still* hold on? This "buy and hold" stuff is fine if you're Rip van Winkle, but not so easy if you're human.

So like any rule, this one is meant to be applied with common sense. The U.S. stock market, which makes new highs every day as I write this, is not Japan in 1990. But if I had just come into some big bucks, I wouldn't rush to dump it all into the market. We *know* there will be another bear market. There have *always* been bear markets. No harm in holding some cash on the sidelines. The higher the market climbs since the last really bad scare, the more cash you might hold.

But except with the funds you have stashed under the umbrella of a tax-deferred account, any skill you might have "timing the market"—knowing when to be in and when out—will be more than wiped out by the cost of paying capital gains taxes along the way. Warren Buffett is America's second richest man, worth about $30 billion, and perhaps its leading capital-gains tax avoider. He's held his stock in GEICO since the 1950s and in the Washington Post Company since the 1960s. Consider this: if he had turned over his portfolio once a year while getting the same astonishing pre-tax investment returns, he'd be worth barely $3 billion.

Impossible? Well, look at it this way: Buffett's managed to compound his money at roughly 26% a year for four decades. At that rate, $1 grows to $10,000. But chop taxes out of that 26% annual return (using a 28% tax rate, which cuts the return to a "mere" 18.7%), and that same $1 grows to just $950.

5. **Diversify over several stocks in different industries.** If all your money is riding on two or three stocks, you are exposed to far more risk than if you've diversified over 12 or 15 (which should be enough!). And, because stocks of companies within the same industry tend to move together, you will only be truly diversified if you choose from among different sectors of the economy. A program of periodic investments in no-load mutual funds is for many people the easiest, most practical way to achieve diversification—and the most prudent.

   But if you do throw the darts yourself . . .

6. **Ignore the noise.** If there's anything that makes it difficult to succeed in stocks, it's that investors can see how they're doing throughout the day. Stocks move up and down all the time, but that doesn't mean there is significance to every move. John Maynard Keynes, who was not only an economist but also an enormously successful stock market investor, suggested that "One must not allow one's attitude to securities which have a daily market quotation to be disturbed by this fact. Some Bursars will buy without a tremor unquoted and unmarketable investments in real estate which, if they had a selling quotation [regularly available], would turn their hair grey." Just because it's easy to buy and sell stocks on a moment's notice, or get an up-to-the-minute quote, doesn't mean you should. Your time would be better spent trying to figure out what the heck a Bursar was.

7. **Be wary of high-fliers and stocks that "everyone" likes,** even though they may be the stocks of outstanding companies. Their hefty multiples (price/earnings ratios) discount earnings growth far into the future. Which is to say that even if the growth comes in on schedule, the stocks may not go up. They're already up. Should earnings not continue to grow as expected, such stocks can

collapse, even though the underlying company may remain sound. What's more, it can hardly be argued that these stocks have been ignored and that they therefore represent some hidden value Wall Street has failed to discover.

Twenty-odd years ago, I attended an *Institutional Investor* conference—1,000 money managers representing billions upon billions of dollars. The men and women who really move the market. One of the panel sessions was devoted exclusively to ITT. The seminar organizer hadn't been able to find anyone bearish on the stock, so three of the panelists were bullish and the fourth volunteered to play devil's advocate.

Well, when I heard their discussions, and saw all the heads nodding in the audience—at 1,000 shares a nod, I figured—I got this very guilty rush of adrenaline. What if I ran out of the room, rushed to the pay phone, and bought ITT? Would that be a misuse of inside information? I decided it would not, and that's exactly what I did. At $44 a share. Any fool could see that at least a few in the audience would do much the same thing after the meeting, or certainly when they got back to their desks. If they were not interested in ITT stock, why were they sitting through this seminar? And as there was no opposition meeting going on that I knew of persuading an equal number of people to rush to the phones and sell, I figured there would just have to be buying pressure on the stock. How could I miss?

The stock went straight down to 12.

Apparently, they had all put ITT in their portfolios and were now waiting for it to go up. But there was no one left to buy it.

Why invest in companies nobody's ever heard of when you can invest in General Motors, IBM, Coke, or Exxon? Why not the best? For one thing, you pay a premium for this peace of mind. For another, the peace of mind you get is at least partly illusory. True, these companies are financially all but impregnable. But their stocks can go down almost as much as any other. General Motors was $113 a share in 1965, $29 nine years later.

One of the rare investors who stands out from the crowd is John Marks Templeton, a deeply religious former Rhodes scholar who has managed to beat the Dow by an average of 8% a year since the thirties. A dollar invested in the Templeton Growth Fund at the end of 1954 was worth around $80 when he retired from active management of the fund in 1987. "Because John felt that God was with him," one associate asserts, "he invested with incredible boldness. The results make me think maybe he's right—maybe God is with him." Even more instrumental in his success than the Lord, however, may have been his relentless insistence on value, wherever he had to go to find it. He bought European stocks after World War II, convinced that the Marshall Plan would cause business abroad to boom. At one time fully three-fourths of his fund was invested in Japanese stocks, because stocks there were selling at much lower price/earnings ratios than stocks in the United States. When those p/e's rose dramatically, Templeton shifted his equally dramatic profits to countries offering better values. It takes special initiative and courage to do what no one else is doing. But it can pay off.

8. **Beware the deceptive p/e.** The price/earnings ratio is the guide most investors use to get a quick fix on a stock. It is listed in the paper every day. The p/e tells you how much *p* (price) you have to pay for $1 of this wallet's *e* (earnings).

However, the best the newspaper can do is calculate the p/e based on that day's price and last year's earnings. What you are buying is the right to share in next year's and future years' earnings. It would have done you little good to know, in 1977, that Chrysler, at 16½, was selling at just 3 times its most recent year's earnings, when the following years' earnings turned out to be massive losses. The low p/e was deceptive. It would have done you equally little good, not long after, when Chrysler was 3, to note its astronomical p/e. (A $3 stock earning a penny a share sells at 300 times earnings.) Once the company recovered, it turned out its $3 price had been less than *one* times its future annual earnings.

Thus it's necessary to keep the p/e figure in perspective, taking an average of the last *several* years' earnings and thinking more in terms of the future than the past. This is particularly true with companies—autos, cement, construction, paper, and many others—whose profits rise and fall in cycles.

9. **Don't waste money subscribing to investment letters or expensive services.** The more-expensive investor newsletters and computer services only make sense for investors with lots of money—if then. Besides their cost, there is the problem that they are liable to tempt you into buying, and scare you into selling, much too often, thereby incurring much higher brokerage fees and capital gains taxes than you otherwise might. There is the added problem that half the experts, at any given time, are likely to be wrong. Indeed, there is one letter which simply analyzes the sentiment of all the others—and advises you to do the opposite, on the not-unreasonable theory that when most of the services are bullish, it's time to sell, and vice versa.

You want to know my idea of real market brilliance? A well-heeled former associate editor of *Forbes,* now back in the business world, sold all his stocks the day before the market began a rapid 10% slide. It was pure genius. I was green with envy and admiration.

"Peter, how did you know?" I asked him, making a mental note to pay better heed to his opinions in the future.

"I needed the cash to buy my apartment," he said.

You can tell a lot about most publicly traded companies just by obtaining the current issue of the

Standard & Poor's monthly *Stock Guide*. Many brokers give it to their clients for free.

This little booklet provides key facts about almost any company you are likely to invest in: its ticker symbol; where it's traded; how many institutions own a piece; how much they own; what business the company is in; how the stock has performed over the last 12, 36, and 60 months; the price/earnings ratio; dividend yield; how long a dividend has been paid; and some sketchy balance-sheet and earnings figures. One column even gives letter grades to the quality of the company's growth and stability of its earnings and dividends.

You could spend many hours writing for past annual reports, reading footnotes, consulting your accountant, even visiting the company and testing its products—but much of what you will ever know about a company you can find out in 60 seconds with the *Stock Guide*. In three minutes more, you can read the one-page summary sheet Standard & Poor's puts out on just about every public company. Brokers happily fax them over, if asked. Or stop by your local library. Not to mention the wealth of information now available cheaply by computer. Through the Internet you can get instant SEC filings (**www.sec.gov/edgarhp.htm**), free real-time stock quotes (**www.thomsonrtq.com**), tons of stock and mutual fund information (**www.morningstar.net**), and lots, lots more (see **www.investorama.com**).

But you know what? You could drown in all this information. Far better, if you ask me, to stick to *Forbes* and *Barron's*. The editors of these magazines have always stressed a level-headed, value-oriented approach to investing. They frequently run stories on companies, or whole lists of companies, that seem to be undervalued (or overvalued). Any one of them will give you more good investment ideas than you'll possibly have time or money to pursue. For a few dollars a year, you can get the services of several dozen financially sophisticated editors, writers, and columnists. In fact, if you just bought the first three or four issues of *Barron's* each year—for its annual expert "roundtable"—you'd have spent $10 or so to get more than enough good ideas.

10. **Invest—don't speculate.** It's one thing to take risks in low-priced stocks that you hope, over time, may work out their problems and quintuple in value. That's a kind of speculation I admit to having a weakness for. If you can afford the risk, it may reward you handsomely. But it's quite another thing to jump in and out of stocks (or options or futures) hoping to "play the market" successfully. Every time you jump, your broker cuts down your stake. Even if you're using a deep discounter, where the commission is trivial, there is also the "spread" to contend with—what costs 12⅛ if you're buying often fetches just 12 if you're selling. And for any profits, there is that meat cleaver: taxes.

Buy value and hold it. Don't switch in and out. Don't try to outsmart the market.

11. **Sell only when a stock has gone up so much that you feel it no longer represents a good value.** Don't sell because you think business or the market generally is going to get bad, because:

❖ if you think so, chances are lots of other people think so, too, and the market may already have discounted this possibility (that is, the stock price may already reflect it);

❖ you could be wrong;

❖ even if business does get bad, someday it will get better—and in the meantime you are collecting dividends rather than paying brokerage commissions and capital gains taxes.

12. **If you have both taxable and tax-sheltered portfolios, keep your riskiest holdings outside your tax-sheltered accounts.** Risky stocks—and risky mutual funds—can produce losses that, up to $3,000 a year, reduce your taxable income. Those losses are *wasted* inside an IRA

or some other tax-deferred account. Conversely, the huge gains you will occasionally reap from your riskiest holdings are favored with long-term capital gains treatment if held directly by you and for more than a year. Inside a tax-sheltered account, they get no such treatment. They will be taxed as ordinary income when withdrawn. It's the less speculative, dividend-and-interest-paying securities, for the most part, that you should stick in your tax-sheltered accounts.

CHAPTER 8

Choosing (to Ignore) Your Broker

What always impresses me is how much better the relaxed, long-term owners of stocks do with their portfolios than the traders do with their switching of inventory. The relaxed investor is usually better informed and more understanding of essential values; he is more patient and less emotional; he pays smaller annual capital gains taxes; he does not incur unnecessary brokerage commissions; and he avoids behaving like Cassius by "thinking too much."

—LUCIEN O. HOOPER,
Forbes

Wait a minute (you say). You've told me all this but you haven't told me the part about choosing a brilliant but level-headed, highly experienced, and highly ethical broker. Where's the part about him? If I can find a guy who knows how to make money in the market, and who spends all day at it, why do I have to know about anything but how to retire?

There is a bit in a Woody Allen movie where Woody is standing in line, and a man behind him is lecturing his date, loudly and pretentiously, about Marshall McLuhan. Finally, Woody turns and says (in effect): "I don't know why you're talking so loud, but since you are I have to tell you I think you've got McLuhan all wrong." "Oh, yeah?" says the other man. "Well, I just happen to *teach a course* on McLuhan at Columbia." "Well, that's funny," says Allen, unfazed, "because *I* just happen to have McLuhan right here." Whereupon he goes behind a prop and pulls out Marshall McLuhan. McLuhan looks at the man and says dryly: "You know nothing of my work. How you ever got to teach a course in anything is totally amazing."

Woody Allen looks straight into the camera, at us, and says: "Boy, if life were only like this!"

Indeed, I have terrible news about brokers and money managers generally—news which I expect you've suspected, but couldn't quite believe, all along. There *are* no brokers who can beat the market consistently and by enough of a margin to more than make up for their brokerage fees. Or, if there are a few, they are not going to work for peanuts—and any account under $100,000 is peanuts. Or if they will—because they are just starting out in business or have a soft spot in their heart for you—*there's no way for you to know who they are*. Even if they can prove to you that they have done very well in the past (not just say it—prove it), that doesn't mean they will do very well in the future.

If you get 256 people into a room and give them each a coin to flip, the odds are that half of them—128—will flip heads on the first try. That is the object, you tell them: to flip heads. Of those 128 winners, 64 will flip heads on the next go-round as well. Twice running. Not bad. Thirty-two people will flip heads three times in a row, sixteen will flip heads four times in a row, eight will flip heads five times in a row, four will succeed six times in a row, two will rack up an incredible seven straight successes, and one—one out of all 256 in the crowd—will flip heads eight times in a row. What talent! What genius!

What nonsense. This man is no more or less likely than anyone else in the room to flip heads the ninth time. His chances are fifty-fifty. He is not a genius, he is a statistic in a probability formula. As is some other man in the crowd of 256 (who may actually *be* a genius) who, odds are, failed eight times running to flip heads.

In any given year, half the stock market players will beat

the averages and half will do worse.* After eight years, one player out of every 256—be he broker or mutual fund, private investor or bank trust department—is likely to have done better than average every single year. (Except that, since we all want to put our best feat forward, chances are that more than one will say he did.)

That player, naturally, will attract quite a following. What talent! What genius!

What nonsense.

I'm not saying the stock market is all luck. Nevertheless, it is enough of a crap shoot that luck has a great deal more to do with it than any professional money man is going to want to admit.

By and large you should manage your *own* money (via no-load mutual funds). No one is going to care about it as much as you. And no one but you is going to manage it for free.

This runs very much against the accepted line. The accepted line is that your money is too important to be managed in your spare time: you should let a full-time professional manage it for you, even though you will have to pay him to do so.

Who are these professionals and how well do they do and what do they charge? How do you find one who has been right eight times running—and *are* his chances any better than anyone else's to be right the ninth time?

I am being driven from a Boston TV station to Harvard Business School by a fellow alumnus, an investment counselor with an outstanding firm. He is paid not to manage money or make trades but to advise people on how to invest.

"My biggest pitch," he says, "is so simple really—it's that clients shouldn't put all their eggs in one basket. I

---

* Actually, more than half will do worse because players pay brokerage commissions and stock market averages don't.

know that sounds like plain common sense you'd learn in the third grade, it's real simple, but that's what I'm paid to advise." He is paid many tens of thousands of dollars a year; his services are billed out to clients at two or three times that price. He advises Big Money. He recommends utilities on TV *after* they've doubled in price (maybe they'll double again?). Welcome to the world of professional money management.

Item: On June 30, 1967, the publisher, editor-in-chief and editor of *Forbes* magazine mounted the *New York Times* stock pages on the wall. They threw ten darts apiece, tried again with the darts that missed the pages altogether, and invested a hypothetical $1,000 in each dart-selected stock. Fifteen years later, by 1982, the portfolio had appreciated 239%. Over the same period, the Standard & Poor's 500 rose just 35%, and many money managers hadn't done even that well.

Item: Computer Directions Advisors, Inc., a Maryland financial consulting firm, programmed a computer to choose 100 different portfolios of 15 stocks apiece—*at random*—from the 2,700-odd stocks on the New York and American stock exchanges. *Eighty-two* of the 100 randomly selected portfolios did better than the S&P 500 over the ten years from 1967 to 1976. Ninety-nine of them beat the S&P 500 in 1976. Concluded *Money* magazine: "These results suggest that it pays to look—as the computer did—beyond the large, intensively analyzed companies in the S&P 500." It was, quite simply, a time when smaller-company stocks were outperforming larger ones—as in many time periods they do—and the darts hit lots of smaller companies along with the larger ones in the S&P 500.

Item: On February 28, 1977, the *Wall Street Journal* reported that, "judging by the results of the pooled investment funds banks and insurance companies run, more than three-fourths of the professional managers failed to do as well as the market averages over the past two years. In fact, fewer than one-fourth of them have achieved results as good as or better than the averages, whether for the past year, the past two years or the past four or eight years."

You see the same kind of story year after year. It's not that professional money managers are dumber or lazier than average—just that the market averages don't have to pay brokerage commissions or advisory fees, and so generally outperform people, or institutions, that do.

What is significant is that among money managers there are exceedingly few who consistently do substantially better than their fellows (or substantially worse). This year's winners may be next year's losers.

In school you can pretty well assume that an "A" student this year is likely to do well next year. Not so among money managers. They will flip heads a few years in a row ... but they are just about as likely to flip tails the next. On Wall Street, it is not enough to be smart and hardworking. There are a great many smart, hardworking people on Wall Street. Smart is taken for granted. Lucky is the way to get rich. (The other way is to be a broker.) Inside information doesn't hurt, either.

As for the not-inconsiderable number of dumb people on Wall Street (and in "Wall Street" I include the entire network of electronic tributaries flowing from all over the world into the mighty Manhattan delta), their existence is undeniable. Which naturally gives rise to the question, If They're So Dumb, How Come They're Still in Business? But this just proves my point: Investment success has at least as much to do with luck, patience, psychological balance (unconflicted greed, for example, versus unrelenting guilt and masochism), and inside information (you don't have to be a genius to be well connected) as it does with intelligence.

If the professionals do no better than darts—and most do not—then how much is it worth to have them manage your money?

The answer is that you are probably better off minimizing your "overhead"—investing in index funds (see

Chapter 10) or, if you choose to buy individual stocks, paying as little as possible in brokerage and advisory fees. But before we get to discount brokers, it's worth spending some time discussing a theory that has caused much wringing of hands on Wall Street. It is called *random walk,* and to the extent that it is valid it helps to explain why professionals are just as apt to blunder as you or I. That is, after all, an intuitively unpalatable notion.

The random walk theory holds that you cannot predict the price of a stock by looking back at charts that show where it has been ("technical analysis") or by studying the business prospects of the underlying company ("fundamental analysis"). On any given day, a given stock—or the market as a whole—is as likely to go up as down.

The reason, according to this theory, is that the stock market is "efficient." As soon as a new bit of information becomes known about a company (or the world), it is reflected almost immediately in the price of the stock (or the market). By the time that bit of information filters down to you or me or much of anyone else, it is already reflected in the price of the stock. It has been "discounted."

True, if you happen to be the daughter of the judge who is presiding over a $900 million antitrust suit brought by a tiny computer firm against Microsoft, and if no one on Wall Street is taking the suit at all seriously, but your daddy has just told you he's going to surprise the pants off those bastards at Microsoft and award the full $900 million to the little computer company . . . well, then you could probably profit quite handsomely by buying stock in the little computer company. (You could also get yourself and your daddy into very hot water.) You have inside information.

But, inside information apart (and believe me, if you're hearing it from your broker or the company's sales manager's brother-in-law, it's no longer inside information— everyone and his brother has heard it), the market, according to the random walk theory, efficiently digests all the information available to it.

Thus when a company announces higher earnings, the stock may go up—or it may sit pat or even decline. It depends how those higher earnings compare with what the market was expecting. It's not enough to buy Bethlehem Steel thinking that, with an upturn in the economy, steel profits will be good. If *you* think that, chances are lots of other people have already thought so, too, and the possibility is already reflected in the price. Only if the gain proves more than expected will the price rise.

So you not only have to know what profits will be—you also have to try to figure out how that compares with what other people expect. Which gives you not just one but two chances to guess wrong. Between 1967 and 1982, IBM profits sextupled and its dividend grew eightfold. Yet a share of IBM was actually worth less in July 1982 than in December 1967. It finally did move to new highs as the 1982 bull market took hold, but fifteen years is a long time to wait.

Choosing a horse, you just have to guess which one will run the fastest. With a stock, you have to guess how well a company will do, whether that will make the stock go up or down, and which way the track itself (the market) is moving. (The advantage in owning a stock is that the race doesn't end. You don't have to sell the stock until you want to . . . you *own* something. If you have chosen a good value, you will receive dividends, share in future growth, and, with any luck, ultimately be vindicated.)

The random walk theory naturally is anathema to the men and women whose livelihoods and self-esteem depend on convincing clients they know which way stock prices will go. Many studies have been undertaken to refute it. It is in connection with these studies that computers are made to simulate dart-throwing monkeys. Yet the evidence is that it is exceptionally rare for anyone regularly to beat the averages to any meaningful degree.

Burton Malkiel, a professor at Princeton drafted by President Ford to sit on the three-man Council of Economic Advisers, wrote an excellent stock market guide called *A*

Random Walk Down Wall Street. In it he made a tight case for random walk, citing numerous rigorously designed and executed studies. Yet he remained himself "a random walker with a crutch." He argued that random walk theory does not have to be absolutely right or wrong. It is *largely* right. It is *largely* true that you can't outguess the market. And it is particularly difficult to outguess the market by enough to justify the transaction costs you will incur by switching in and out.

David Dreman, author of *The New Contrarian Investment Strategy,* writing in *Barron's,* made a good case against random walk. He pointed out that stock markets have always been irrational and concluded that a rational man could therefore outdo the herd. "Market history gives cold comfort to the Random Walkers," he writes. "'Rational' investors in France, back in 1719, valued the Mississippi Company at 80 times all the gold and silver in the country—and, just a few months later, at only a pittance."

It is true, I think, that by keeping one's head and sticking to value, one may do better than average. But it's not easy. Because the real question is not whether the market is rational but whether by being rational we can beat it. Had Dreman been alive in 1719, he might very reasonably have concluded that the Mississippi Company was absurdly overpriced at, say, three times all the gold and silver in France. And he might have shorted some. At six times all the gold and silver in France he might have shorted more. At twenty times all the gold and silver in France he might have been ever so rational—and thoroughly ruined. It would have been cold comfort to hear through the bars of debtors' prison that, some months later, rationality had at last prevailed. A driveling imbecile, on the other hand, caught up in the crowd's madness, might have ridden the stock from three times to eighty times all the gold and silver in France and, quite irrationally, struck it rich.

There are rare individuals who can consistently outperform the market. Peter Lynch. Warren Buffett. And they poke big holes in the random walk theory, however valid it may be for most investors buying and selling widely followed stocks. You can read books about Lynch, who ran Fidelity's Magellan Fund with such astonishing success, or about Buffett, who became the second richest man in America with shrewd investments through his Berkshire Hathaway Corporation. But knowing how they did it is different from being able to do it yourself. Nor is it likely to help you find the *next* Peter Lynch or the *next* Warren Buffett.* Unfortunately, choosing a winning investment advisor, even if you can afford his services, is not much easier than choosing a winning stock.

Choosing a winner *broker* will be even harder. Unlike an investment advisor, a broker spends much of his time on the phone selling to new clients, selling to old clients, giving stock quotes and up-to-the-moment market appraisals, talking sports, talking politics, making excuses for recommendations that have gone sour—or handling paperwork, seeing that trades get made, and straightening out back-office snafus. He has little time to search out exceptional values or to formulate broad economic and financial

---

* Actually, at this writing, the current Warren Buffett is very much alive and well, and you can buy shares in his company—stock symbol BRK—just by picking up the phone and calling any broker. But you've missed a lot of the run. When I *first* thought the stock was a little ahead of itself, 20-odd years ago, it was $300 a share, up from $19 in 1965. Today it's still a little ahead of itself: $70,000 a share.

I have long rued my folly in failing to buy—and ruminated on possible explanations for his success. How to explain it? The way I see it, Warren Buffett is smarter and wiser than almost anybody . . . completely single-minded in his efforts . . . aided by his equally clear-sighted and extraordinary partner Charlie Munger . . . boosted by the financial leverage in his shrewd insurance businesses (he gets to invest the premiums until you crash your car or the earthquake hits) . . . and the beneficiary, by now, of three special advantages: people all take his calls; potential acquirees enjoy a certain cachet and might accept a lower price in Berkshire stock than in the stock of just any old company; once Buffett invests/anoints, the world follows. So Buffett is clearly real—but an exception. Still, we can all learn a lot from his example. Buffett almost never traded in-and-out, never made a nickel that I know of buying puts and calls . . . it's been good, thoughtful, patient investing, with a great premium placed on the quality of management.

views, as investment advisors and money managers theoretically do.

And unlike an investment advisor, who takes a set annual fee for his services, a broker only makes money when you trade in or out of a stock. Eager as a broker may be to see your account prosper, that is not his first interest. With rare exceptions (and all brokers will claim to be that rare exception), his first interest is to do well himself. His first interest is commissions to feed his family. His first interest is hitting the bonus level at the end of the month that will pay for his family's trip to Disney World. He is as anxious as any salesman that you be pleased with your purchase—more so, because the better you do, the more money you will have to make future purchases—but his first interest is to make the sale. He will never tell you this, but you should never forget it.

Which reminds me:

13. **Never buy anything from a broker who calls you up cold.** This is so basic as not to warrant elaboration.

If most brokers are wrong as often as they are right (and they are), if the market is *largely* a random walk and if *Forbes* and *Barron's* are likely to do as well for you as a team of personal advisors (at a tiny fraction of the price), then why do you need a broker at all?

You need him to execute your trades, to give you stock quotes, to allow you to buy stocks on margin, to hold your certificates, to mail your dividend checks and monthly statements and annual reports—*and all these services are available from "discount brokers" at discounts ranging up to 90%.* And from "deep discounters," who make trading almost free. What they will not do is hold your hand, give you bad advice (or good), or try to sell you anything.

A discount broker won't call you in the middle of the day—in the middle of a root canal, if you are a dentist—to tell you the bad news that's just come over the tape about one of your stocks.

But that's good.

Had he called, you might have panicked into selling. In so many cases, seemingly dreadful news turns out to be news everyone expected, or news about a Brazilian subsidiary that accounts for 3% of the company's sales, or news that pales beside the good news that will be announced the following week. If it's really important news, and no one expected it, the stock will be shut down from trading before you can sell, anyway; and when it reopens, sharply lower, the new price will reflect investors' assessment of the news.

With a discount broker, you won't rush into making unnecessary trades. You can finish the root canal in peace.

There is an old joke on Wall Street. "Well," the joke goes, "the broker made money and the firm made money—and two out of three ain't bad." I have heard this joke, often, from a broker with an unobstructed view of the Statue of Liberty and a number of important institutional accounts. One of these accounts entrusted his firm with $175,000 for a flier in options. The institution was shrewd in its timing, as it turned out. The stock market rallied dramatically. Never could one have made as much in options as then. Yet in two months, through an elaborate series of computer-assisted ins, outs, and straddles, the firm's options trader managed to turn that $175,000 into $10,000—generating $87,000 in commissions along the way.

Anyway, if you are already "in the market," making occasional trades, my first suggestion—if you can bear to do it—is that you go through last year's confirmation slips to see what you paid in commissions. You may be surprised. I didn't know I churned my own account, either. Next to rent, it turned out that brokerage commissions were my biggest expense in life.

Adding up one's commissions is a calculation rarely performed. Computerized monthly brokerage statements leave the figure tactfully untallied.

If it turns out you didn't spend much on brokerage commissions last year, fine. But if you are unpleasantly surprised, as I was, I have another suggestion. Not a silly suggestion like "stop churning your account"—a practical suggestion that allows you to enjoy your little vice for less. Switch your account to a deep-discount broker.

Depending on your relationship with your current broker, this may be easier said than done. My own full-price broker is probably the best in his mid-Manhattan office. The brightest, the most personable, the busiest. Our typical phone conversation used to go like this:

VOICE: Mr. ———'s office. *(Already this was ridiculous because he had neither an office nor a secretary, so this just meant both his hands had phones in them and he couldn't pick up a third.)*

ME *(playing along)*: Is Mr. ——— in?

VOICE: One moment, please.

HIM: Hello?

ME: Who was that who answered the ph—

HIM: Can you hold on a minute?

(All I want to know is one stock quote, but I want to know it badly enough to hold on.)

HIM: Hi.

ME: Hi. How am I doing?

HIM: Fine, thanks, how are *you*?

ME: Fine. How's my stock?

HIM: Not very . . . can you hold on a minute?

(Silence)

HIM: Can you believe that guy? He's short 500 Xerox and . . .

Eventually I got my quote, but it took some doing. Getting a whole list of quotes could be like sitting through a soap opera waiting for the plot tidbits. To keep me listening, once in a while he would throw me a quote.

The problem was, we'd become friends. Because we're friends, I resent it if he's busy when I call. And because I work for a living, I resent it if I'm busy when *he* calls.

What's ludicrous is that, because we're friends, he resents it if *I'm* busy when he calls.

So it boils down to this: I wouldn't drop my broker any more than I'd drop any other good friend. And over the years this has cost me a small fortune. Three such friends and I'd be out on the street.

I've been paying him to listen to my troubles, and I've been paying to listen to his troubles. The fact is, I think my troubles are more interesting than his, and I think my investment advice is as good—so why isn't he paying me? We have often discussed that very point, and he couldn't agree with me more, and I keep paying him (although I now also deal with a discount broker, and a deep discounter, and don't have to beg for stock quotes—I have a computer).

14. **Minimize your transaction costs.** Unless yours has consistently outperformed the market, in which case you won't believe any of this anyway, you should shop around for the cheapest broker. (See page 221.) You will save hundreds or thousands of dollars in commissions and lose little or nothing. I repeat: Most discounters perform all the services of a regular broker, minus the advice and the personality. Full-rate brokers will claim that they provide better executions on trades—that they get you better prices than discount brokers can. But there's no evidence to support this, especially as regards trades of just a few hundred or a few thousand shares.

    You can even use a discount broker to buy no-load mutual funds. You won't save any money, because no-loads already carry no sales charge. In fact, there can be a small processing fee (though quite a few funds have arranged with the largest discounters to have it waived). But there are advantages. You can buy and sell funds with a simple phone call (no applications to fill out and mail), switch easily from one fund to another even if they're from different fund "families," avoid worrying about minimum purchases, and get one consolidated statement for tax purposes. Through a discounter you're also able to borrow against the value of your funds or buy them on margin (careful!). And you have access to the cash-management accounts some discounters offer, with check-writing privileges.

So Why Not Hire a Monkey?

Does all this mean a monkey could handle your financial planning? No. It takes intelligence to match your financial strategy with your circumstances: how much risk you can afford, what time horizons you are looking at, what tax bracket you are in. It takes intelligence to try to perceive value. A monkey might buy municipal bonds for a Keogh Plan—but that's like throwing money out the window.* A monkey might buy growth stocks for an 80-year-old widow who needs a secure income. A monkey might buy Avon at 60 times earnings as the Morgan Guaranty Trust Company and so many others did.

A monkey does not have what investing well really takes: common sense.

---

* Why accept a lower yield for a tax-free bond for an account that isn't subject to current taxation anyway—and in effect turn it into a taxable bond, since the income it produces *will* eventually be taxed when you withdraw it?

CHAPTER 9

Hot Tips, Inside Information—and Other Fine Points

If you bet on a horse, that's gambling. If you bet you can make three spades, that's entertainment. If you bet cotton will go up three points, that's business. See the difference?

—BLACKIE SHERRODE
as quoted by James Dines in *Technical Analysis*

Hot Tips

Here is what to do with hot tips. If you get a hot tip, make a note of it and pretend to be very interested. But don't buy. If the thing takes off, listen a little more closely the next time this fellow has a tip. If it gets mauled, look bitter the next time you see him. He will assume that you bought the stock; he will feel guilty; and he will buy you a very nice lunch.

Annual Reports

Annual reports are organized very simply. The good news is contained up front in the president's message and ensuing text; the bad news is contained in the footnotes to the financial statement.

You should be aware that for big, widely followed companies, everything of any substance contained in the annual report was known to sophisticated investors months earlier.

Inside Information

It's much easier (although illegal) to make money in the market with inside information than with annual reports.

A Republican I know in the executive suite at a major insurance company called a close friend of his in a distant city (a Democrat) and told him to buy all he could of a company then selling at $6 a share. Several days later, the insurance giant tendered for the company at $10 a share. The Republican and the Democrat quietly split the profit. A lot of money is made this way on Wall Street, hard though the SEC tries to prevent it.

Or say you are a trader with a major firm and you get a call from one of the big banks asking you to buy 500,000 shares of Guess?, Inc., the blue jeans people. That's a lot of stock. It will in all likelihood move the price of Guess? up a point or two, at least temporarily. You have this friend somewhere you owe a favor and, when you bump into him, you mention that Guess? sure looks good for a quick move. He buys options on the stock and doubles his money in two days. Now he owes you a favor.

Unfortunately, very few investors are anywhere near close enough to the center of financial power ever to be tempted by genuine inside information.*

Charts

Charts look like they should work, but they don't. Everybody uses them anyway, just as everyone consults astrology

---

* Or perhaps I should say "fortunately." A lot of people who never dreamed they could get caught have been—and some have even gone to jail.

columns in newspapers. Some people even take them seriously. Much good may it do them. The various precepts, strategies, systems, rules of thumb, and general folklore that chart readers espouse have been rigorously tested. To quote Malkiel: "The results reveal conclusively that past movements in stock prices cannot be used to foretell future movements [any more than past flips of a coin will help determine the next flip]. The stock market has no memory. The central proposition of charting is absolutely false, and investors who follow its precepts will accomplish nothing but increasing substantially the brokerage charges they pay. Yes," Malkiel writes, "history does tend to repeat itself in the stock market, but in an infinitely surprising variety of ways that confound any attempts to profit from a knowledge of past price patterns."

Nonetheless, chartists are likely to be right about as often as they are wrong, and so constantly find new reasons to believe in their craft. The bookshelves bulge.

Don't waste your time.

Splits

Splits are accorded great excitement on Wall Street. Before the split you had just 200 shares of the stock, at $40 each ($8,000). Now—presto!—you have *400* shares of the stock, at $20 each (still $8,000). Nothing has happened; your share of the pie is exactly what it was. They have exchanged your dollars for twice as many half-dollars or four times as many quarters or ten times as many dimes.

The advantages corporations hope to gain from splits are: to lower the price of the stock so more people can afford to buy it in round lots; to make it look "cheaper"; to increase the number of shares outstanding, and hence the trading volume and liquidity of the stock.

Although splits can affect a stock's price, at least temporarily, they in no way change a stock's underlying value (or lack thereof).

Stock Dividends

The only difference between a stock dividend and a stock split is that, being a very *small* split, it is hoped no prospective buyers will even notice it has taken place.

Stock dividends are under no circumstances to be confused with real dividends. Their (dubious) value is entirely psychological—it is hard to believe that it merits the cost of adjusting everyone's records and answering the questions of confused shareholders.

Prior to the dividend, 100% of the company was divided among the shareholders. Then, in an attempt to keep those shareholders happy without having to pay them anything, each one is given 3% more shares. Now they have exactly what they had before—100% of the company. It is just divided into slightly smaller pieces.

You pay no tax on a stock dividend, because it adds no value to your holdings. What you hope, however, is that Wall Street will not notice that your company has made this quiet little "split" and, accordingly, will keep paying what it used to pay for each now-slightly-less-valuable share.

Sometimes it actually works.

Dividend Reinvestment Plans

These are not the same as stock dividends. Many big companies give their shareholders the choice of receiving their (real) dividend either in cash or in stock. Either way you have to declare the full amount as income. But if you choose to take stock instead of cash, the company takes your dividend, along with a lot of others, and either goes into the market and buys its own stock for you with your money or else sells it direct to you from the corporate treasury.

The advantages to you are that you are forced to save money you might otherwise have spent—if you consider that an advantage—and you pay no brokerage commission to buy the stock. Often, you even get a 5% discount.

The advantage to the company is that it helps keep the stock up (if purchased in the open market) or raises new capital without having to pay underwriting fees and going through lengthy SEC prospectus procedures (if sold from the corporate treasury).

Although there is no harm in taking dividends in stock—for small investors it's actually quite a good deal—it makes more sense for substantial investors to take the cash and then decide the optimum place to put it.

Selling Short

When you sell a stock you don't own, you are "selling short." You do this if you think a stock is likely to go down and you wish to profit from its misfortune. To sell a stock short you instruct your broker to (a) "borrow" it from someone who does own it, (b) sell it, and then, eventually, (c) buy it back—hopefully at a lower price than you sold it for—so that you can (d) return it. Buying it back to return it is called "covering" your short position.

Selling short is not un-American, as some people seem to feel, but it carries with it three problems. First, a relatively small one, is that instead of *receiving* dividends while you sit with your position, you may actually have to *pay* them. (You borrowed the stock from some nameless, faceless person who does not even know it's been lent; then you sold the stock; now the company pays a 40-cent-a-share dividend, which the lender naturally expects to receive. Your broker deducts that amount from your account and deposits it in his. Silver lining: any dividends you pay lower your taxable income.)

Second, by selling short you are in effect betting against the management of a company, who are doubtless applying their best efforts to making things turn out all right. They could succeed. (Actually, you are betting that *other* investors have not fully grasped how feeble management's competence really is, or what a mess the company is really in, or how little value really underlies its inflated stock, and thus are willing to pay you more for it, when you sell it, than they should.)

Third and most serious, shorting stocks makes the amateur investor even more nervous than buying them. It is not at all atypical for the small investor to spot a stock that is genuinely worth shorting, short it, begin to go crazy as it climbs yet another 20 points, lose his resolve, and bail out at the top—just days before the bottom falls out.

This can even happen to big investors. One man of my acquaintance observed the wild rise in gambling stocks occasioned by the development of Atlantic City and shorted Resorts International, wildest of the bunch. He shorted a lot. And it went up a lot. But this gentleman is nothing if not confident in his acumen, and so he left the country for a six-month round-the-world jaunt, short many thousands of shares of Resorts International, checking in with his brokers every so often by phone. Each time he checked in, from country after country, Resorts was higher. The bubble, against all reason, refused to burst. It is easy to say with hindsight that, had he held on for just a few countries more, the bubble would indeed have burst (all bubbles do) and all his paper losses would soon have been erased. But there in the Australian outback (or wherever) it had begun to look to my friend as though he might actually lose everything. Discretion being the better part of valor, he decided to cut his losses—$19 million—and cover his short position. That was, of course, the top.

It was a rare mistake for this remarkably successful investor, but a useful tale for the rest of us.

With shorts you are swimming against the tide of the brokerage commission you have to pay, the dividends you may have to pay, the market's long-term upward bias, the efforts of management, your own psychological frailties (like getting scared), your own financial limits (like running out of cash to meet your margin calls as the stock rises, so you *have to* take your loss, even though you wanted to hold on), and—should you actually make a profit—the lack of any long-term capital gains break for short-sale profits, no matter how long you've held your short.

Final caution: If you do want to short a stock, never short it "at the market." When you buy or sell "at the market," you are instructing your broker to pay whatever he has to, or accept whatever he has to, to make the trade. The alternative to "market orders" are "limit orders." "Buy 100 shares at 38¼ or better," you tell your broker, meaning that 38¼ is the absolute top you will pay. (You can place limit orders for the "day only," which means that if the broker is unable to make the trade by the end of the day he'll stop trying; or "good-till-canceled," which means you'd better remember to cancel it if you change your mind.)

It is dangerous to short a stock "at the market" because there is a rule about short sales: you may only short a stock on an "uptick"—that is, when the price is higher than the "last different price at which it traded." If the stock is falling apart, it can be some time before there is an uptick. You wanted to short it at 29½, but placed a "market order"; it trades at 29¼, 29¼, 29, 28⅞, then a block at 28½, more at 28⅛, a big block at 27⅜, more at 27¼, 27, 26⅞, 100,000 shares at 26, and, then, finally, somebody bumps it up an eighth—an uptick—and that is where your broker calls to tell you that you shorted the stock. (Had you simply been selling it rather than shorting it, you would have made the sale at around 29¼.)

Place a limit on all short sales. Instruct your broker to sell at some figure—say, 29 "or better"—so that you don't wind up making a trade you wish you hadn't.

Special Offerings

From time to time you may be called upon by your broker to benefit from a "special offering," also known as a "spot secondary." Special offerings are one of the few times where you should consider selling short. Simply put, the special offering is a way of unloading onto the public stock that none of the big professional money managers wants to touch. This is done not by giving the public a good break on the price of a stock, in the great tradition of the white elephant sale, but rather by giving the retail broker a fat incentive to push the stuff on his clients—in the great tradition of the hype.

When the broker calls to sell you National Hypothetical—fine company though it may be—don't buy, *sell*. He will stress that you will incur no brokerage fee if you buy the stock—the seller has generously agreed to pick up the tab—but short it anyway. If the stock hasn't fallen nicely within a week or two, cover the short and call it a day. But in most cases, the stock does fall. Cover your short and pocket a quick profit.

Here is an example of a true-life special offering: 67,000 shares of Witco Chemical. Witco, a sound, prosperous company, had been selling around 32 up until a few days before the offering; the stock was being offered at 30 (of which the seller would receive only about 28½, with the rest going to the brokerage house and the broker).

With a special offering there is no prospectus, no advance warning so investors can study the situation carefully—it's hit-and-run, done overnight and into the next day. The stock continues to trade on the floor of the New York Stock Exchange while brokers are trying to unload their special block off the Exchange.

Witco was actually selling at around 29½ on the open market, a couple of hundred shares at a time, while the brokerage firm was pushing 67,000 shares onto its clients at 30. I managed to short 300 shares. Within a day or two it was 28¾. Then quarterly earnings were announced: $1.09, versus $1.22 for the year-earlier quarter. (Is it possible the sellers of 67,000 shares had an inkling?) Two days later the stock was 26¼.

One reason stocks go down after special offerings is that the people in such a hurry to sell sometimes have a reason. The other is that such a big sale sops up a lot of demand for a stock, leaving a preponderance of potential sellers and a dearth of potential buyers.

I describe special offerings not because they occur very often—they're all but extinct—but as an example of what reputable brokers will do, if necessary, to earn commissions. All 67,000 shares of Witco were sold at 30.

The Counter

If there is really a counter somewhere, I have never seen it. "Over-the-counter" is an arena of stocks too small to be (or just not interested in being) traded on a stock exchange. Instead of there being an "auction" market for these stocks, where buyers and sellers meet to do business, there are dealers who keep them in inventory. You want some, we got some.

The problem with O-T-C stocks, particularly if you're not planning to buy and hold for the long haul, is that in addition to brokerage commissions you have the "dealer spread" to contend with. The dealer spread, in percentage terms, can be enormous. A stock may be quoted at 4½ bid, 5½ asked. That means you have to pay the dealer $550 for 100 shares, plus a commission to your broker; and then you can turn around and sell him the same 100 shares for $450, *minus* a commission for the broker. Although that is about as extreme as the spreads get, and although your broker can often do a little better for you than the listed quote, it is very discouraging. In this example the stock has to rise from 4½ bid to about 6 bid—a 33% gain—just for you to break even.

By now, with the growth of NASDAQ—which didn't even exist when this book first was published—a host of major companies are traded this way, from Apple to Microsoft to Intel, and with them the spread is insignificant. What's more, the SEC has in the last couple of years done some excellent work to narrow spreads. Still, with small, illiquid stocks, you must take their often enormous spreads fully into account before investing.

Portfolio

You have heard of a pride of lions, a medley of ducks, an hysteria of hyenas? So, too, a portfolio of stocks and bonds.

Beta

Beta is a measure of a stock's volatility. When the market goes up, does this stock tend to go up faster? Or not as fast? When the market is falling, does this stock plunge? Or does it just drift downward? The more speculative the stock (or portfolio), the higher its beta. If it moves twice as sharply as the market—a 10% decline in the market produces a 20% decline in the stock—its beta is 2. If it moves only half as forcefully—a 10% market gain produces only a 5% gain in the stock—then its beta is 0.5. Most stocks move about like the market, give or take a little, so most stocks have betas around 1.

It doesn't take calculus to know that utilities are relatively stodgy and that hot technology stocks are more speculative. But beta quantifies it. "What's your portfolio's beta?" you can ask show-off friends to put them in their place. On the off chance they have any idea, you should react this way:

❖ If beta is under 1: "Playing it safe this year, eh?" (Particularly biting if the market has recently been zooming.)

❖ If beta is over 1: "Looking for a good run in the market, are you?"

Beta late than never.
You beta believe it.

The Dow Jones Industrial Average

Against all reason, this highly unscientific average of 30 stocks is probably the most widely followed "financial barometer" in the world—and probably always will be, which is why, reluctantly, I have referred to it throughout this book. (To see where it's been lately, in broad strokes, see the graph on page 172. It shows, as well, how the Dow has fared *adjusted for inflation*. Note that the graph begins in 1966, at a very high point in the market.)

Leverage

Leverage is very boring to write about, because no matter how you attack it, you wind up saying what everyone else says, always, without variation, as sure as the caution on every pack of cigarettes: ". . . but be careful—leverage works both ways."

Leverage is buying a house for $100,000—$20,000 down with an $80,000 mortgage—and selling it, years later, for $140,000. That's not a 40% profit ($40,000 on $100,000); it's a 200% profit ($40,000 on *$20,000*). The difference is leverage. You make a profit not just on your own money but also on the money you borrowed.

Leverage can obviously improve your return on investment. But be careful—leverage works both ways. If you had to sell the house for $80,000—20% less than you paid for it—you'd have just enough to pay back the bank, but not a penny of your own cash left. You'd have lost not 20% on the transaction, but 100%.

Margin

Margin is how brokerage firms make it easy for you to overextend yourself with leverage. They do this by lending you the money to buy more stock than you otherwise could. It's not unlike the credit card a department store will gladly issue, only it's more profitable for the issuer. On small sums the brokerage house will typically charge you 2% more than the banks charge them. Since they hold your stock in their computer as security, they take no risk. If your securities decline in value anywhere near enough to jeopardize the loan, either you ante up more security, or

The Only Other Graph in This Book

Source: Adapted from **Forbes Magazine**

else your position is sold out, like it or not, before it can deteriorate further. (Of course, it is just when others are having their positions sold out from under them that you should be in there with a wheelbarrow, buying.)

Margin Calls

A margin call is what alerts you to the fact that your life is going to hell and that you never should have gotten into the market when you did, let alone on margin.

Options

One way to get incredible leverage is with options.

As if the stock market weren't already enough like Caesars Palace, someone decided the real action would be in trading not stocks, but options. He was right.

Own a stock and you could wait years before it doubles. Buy an option and it can double overnight.

Own a stock and you own a small portion of a company's assets and earning power. Buy or sell an option and you are placing a bet—nothing more.

Options, therefore, are a great deal more fun than stocks, more potentially lucrative, and much more likely to wipe you out. Brokers love them.

If you know which way a stock is going to go, you can make a fortune with options. But the stocks on which options are traded are the most widely followed and intensively analyzed ones . . . the ones most likely to conform to the random walk theory of price movement. The hardest ones to outguess. That being the case, the odds in this game are with your broker.

This doesn't mean that I personally have summoned the willpower to abstain from the options market, or that I would pass up for any sum the opportunity to tell you about the time I bought Merrill Lynch options at ⅜.

There I was at the old Beverly Hills Hotel, in one of the smaller suites (a converted maid's room), charged with writing a story about the litigation over the remake of *King Kong* ("the most exciting original motion picture event of all time," as it was billed) but thinking, instead, about Merrill Lynch.

It was the first week of January 1976, and the market had suddenly begun to go wild. Volume on the New York Stock Exchange, which had been running at an unspectacular 15 or 18 million shares a day, was suddenly hitting 30 million shares. Party to each trade, I knew, were a buyer, a seller—and a broker.

Merrill Lynch stock was selling for around 16½. For some reason it had not yet reacted to the surge in volume. It seemed to me that if the volume kept up, Merrill Lynch stock would rise. So I bought 10 Merrill Lynch April 20s. Which means I purchased 10 options, at 100 shares an option, to buy Merrill Lynch stock at $20 a share (the "strike price"), any time between then and April.

The right to buy a stock for 20 when it is selling at 16½ is not tremendously valuable, so it cost me just ⅜ of a dollar per share—$37.50 per 100-share option—$375 in all. Plus $76.88 in commissions.

Stock market volume continued to surge.

Merrill Lynch stock began to move up.

My options began to move up with it.

God, it was thrilling!

As the stock passed 20—the "strike price"—the option was being traded at 1½. This was the "premium" people were paying for the chance that Merrill Lynch would go still higher before April (possibly much higher) and that the option would thus actually be *worth* something. (Its "intrinsic" value at 20 was still zero. The right to buy something for 20 that *anybody else* can buy at 20 is worth nothing.)

The price I had paid for this option was ⅜. Now it had quadrupled—1½.

I sold two of my options for $300—almost as much as I had paid for all 10. I did this because I am a candy ass.

Stock market volume continued to set records. Why this was happening I had no idea.

I sold two more options at 1¾.

Another at 2¹⁄₁₆.

Two more at 3⅛.

Another at 3⅜ (Merrill Lynch stock was now trading for around 22½).

Another at 5½—$550 for an option that had cost me $37.50.

And, finally, the last at 6.

Total investment: $375. Time elapsed: one month. Profit after commissions (but before taxes): $2,397.67.

Options have a certain allure.

Indeed, had I held all 10 until the April expiration date, instead of selling on the way up, I could have turned my $375 into $15,000!

One thing you have to bear in mind, however, is that somewhere there is a person who sold me those 10 Merrill Lynch April 20s at ⅜.

I won. He lost. Between the two of us, we generated $500 in brokerage commissions.

(I'd like to have given you a more recent example of a triumph I've had with options, but I don't have any. What usually happens with options is that they expire worthless. I could provide lots of examples of *that*.)

Options are what's known as a zero-sum game—for every winner there is an equal and opposite loser—except it's worse than that, because of the brokerage commissions.

The Merrill Lynch options I have been describing are called *calls*. They give the purchaser a call on someone else's stock. If you think a stock is going to go up, you can buy a call on it. If you think it's headed down, you can buy a *put*.

If you buy a put, you are buying the right to sell a stock at a specified price. That right becomes valuable if the stock goes down. Say you buy a General Motors April 70 put. You have the right to sell 100 shares of GM to me (put it to me, as it were) at 70 any time up until April. Say you pay me $50 for this right, and GM is selling at 73. Then camshafts start corroding all over the country and it looks as though GM will have to recall all its cars. The market panics and the stock falls to 51. You buy it at 51 and put it to me at 70. You have made 19 points a share, or $1,900—minus commissions and minus the $50 you paid me for the put.

All you stand to lose when you buy a put is the cost of the put. If you had shorted GM instead, and it had gone to 80, you could have lost a lot more.

We could go on at some length in this vein . . . I have not yet talked of selling puts, just buying them; let alone straddles (buying a put and a call on the same stock at the same time, hoping the stock will make a dramatic move in one direction or another, but not knowing or caring which), spreads (buying an option at one strike price and selling another at a higher or lower strike price), or any of a dozen other arcane strategies one might employ. Applying these strategies, a very sharp CPA friend of mine managed to lose, in one day, October 19, 1987, everything he had managed to make through a decade of patient and intelligent investing in stocks.

If you play the options game as a buyer of puts or calls, you will have some terrific gains, lots of little losses, and lots of brokerage fees. Your broker will stress that you are getting to "control" $16,500 worth of stock (in the case of my 10 Merrill Lynch calls) for a commission of merely $76.88—peanuts. But the fact remains that of the $375 you actually invested—your bet—a little over 20% went to the house. And should you wish to cash in your chips, that's another 20%. The commission rate declines sharply with the size of the trade—and at my deep discounter today would be just $42.50—but it's never insignificant.

Just remember this: it is a zero-sum game and the odds are definitely against you. Anything you do win is fully taxed as a short-term capital gain. There are no dividends, lots of commissions. It may be addictive.

Covered Calls

Say you own 100 shares of IBM, which is trading at 90. You think that at 90 the stock is awfully high; but you think, too, that it's a great company. You really don't want to sell it and have to pay capital-gains tax on your enormous profit (you bought the shares not that long ago at 40), so you do the opposite of buying a call on IBM—you *sell* a call. You give some nameless, faceless buyer the right to buy your 100 shares at, say, 95 any time between now and the third Friday in October. In return, you receive $287.50, less a commission to your broker. This is what's known as "writing a covered call." Should IBM rise above 95 and the call you sold be exercised, you're covered—you have the stock sitting right in your account, waiting to be sent off to its new owner.*

You figure: Hey. I get to keep any appreciation in the stock up to $95. I get to keep the dividend. And now, to light a fire under my rate of return, I get this $287.50! In fact, I get it maybe four times a year, writing 90-day options each time—an extra $1,000 or so a year (after commissions) on my $9,000 of IBM stock. That adds 11% a year to my return!

Writing covered calls is perceived as the conservative way to play the options game, on the intuitively appealing notion that if option buyers lose money, it must be option sellers who make it. But that notion is wrong. It is option *brokers* who make money. The problem with writing covered calls is that you retain virtually all the risk while eliminating all chance of a really exciting gain. What if IBM drops off a cliff and you're still holding it? What good's a lousy $287.50 if the value of your shares drops from $9,000 to $5,750? Or what if IBM shoots from $90 a share to $135? You make the first five points of profit but give up

---

* The truly self-destructive write *naked* calls. With naked calls your gain is limited to the premium you receive; your potential loss is unlimited.

everything from $95 to $135—$4,000 on 100 shares—all in return for that lousy $287.50 (less commission, less taxes).

Like most low-risk gambling systems, writing covered calls works well under ordinary circumstances but kills you at the extremes. It certainly isn't as dumb as buying puts and calls looking for a big profit. But neither is it as smart as some people think.

Commodities

Again? I thought we'd disposed of commodities in the first chapter.

Well, yes—but there is no end to the persistence of the nation's commodities salesmen. I once wrote a very negative column on commodities for *Esquire*. In the ensuing weeks, six different commodities salesmen from as far off as Arkansas (that one touting coffee) called—not to complain, but to try to sell me commodity futures. (What do they know about coffee in Arkansas?)

To reinforce your resolve, I quote from investment veteran John Train's *The Money Masters*:

> Stanley Kroll spent 13 years as a commodity broker. He had about 1,000 nondiscretionary customers [customers who made their own decisions with or without his advice]. . . . He even wrote a book on commodity trading. Stanley Kroll says that none of his original 1,000 customers made money. Not one. . . . Kroll and the other commodity specialists I've talked to agree that the retail commodity speculator will almost always sooner or later lose his money, as infallibly as if he cranked away day and night at a slot machine.

And yet away they crank.

Financial Futures

No longer are you limited to speculating in commodities or currencies like cotton, soybeans, copper, or Swiss francs.

Now you can buy Treasury bond futures, to bet on the direction of interest rates, and stock-index futures, to bet on the direction of the market. And that's just scratching the surface. All of this is loads of fun and, if you know which way interest rates or the market averages are headed, highly profitable. Unfortunately, you don't know which way interest rates or the market averages are heading, and neither do I.

Options on Futures

With futures, you put up a tiny down payment to control vastly more of something than you could ever afford to pay for in full. The leverage is enormous. A modest swing in the price of sugar or gold can make you rich (no problem there) or wipe you out. It was to get around this wipe-out aspect of futures trading that Wall Street—Chicago, actually—invented *options* on futures. With these, you will almost surely lose all you invest, but you can't lose more. Now isn't that terrific? Your loss is limited to the size of your bet. They even have options on Treasury bond and stock-market-index futures. *Come onnnnnnnn, WILLow!*

Penny Stocks

Commonly defined as those selling for under $3 a share, penny stocks fall into two broad categories: those initially issued for just pennies a share—a marketing ploy—and those that became penny stocks against their will.

The former are typically Canadian gold mining stocks and other ventures whose principal merit is that even a poor man can afford to buy 1,000 shares and a dream. They are wildly speculative and burdened by backbreaking spreads. You are all but certain to lose money.

The latter are shares in real companies that have fallen close to or into the arms of bankruptcy, their once-lofty shares commanding just pennies, or at most a few dollars. These are highly speculative investments but sometimes not stupid ones. With Chrysler at 2⅝ (presplit), all you could lose was 2⅝. On the off chance it recovered, you could multiply your money 30-fold. The advantage of these stocks is that, unlike the others, no one is out promoting them. Quite the contrary—everyone is dumping on them. If Wall Street tends to overreact in both directions—and it does—these involuntary penny stocks may sometimes be the object of that overreaction.

Even so, you could lose a lot of money betting on the next Chrysler. The more conservative approach is to invest in a no-load fund like Tweedy, Browne Global Value with a nose for value in the securities of fallen angels.

(It should be noted that a company worth $100 million could just as easily be divided into 1 million $100 shares or 500 million 20-cent shares. By itself, a low share price means nothing. Many British blue chips trade for just a dollar or two a share. In the United States, however, by convention, few healthy, well-regarded companies sell for less than $20, or certainly $10, a share; few tiny speculative companies sell for much over $10.)

Strategic Metals

These are metals like chromium, germanium, and columbium that no thriving military industrial complex should be without. It's just not likely to occur to you to speculate in them—which isn't all that easy, incidentally—when nobody's talking or worrying about them. Only when the world is in an uproar and the prices of these metals are going through the roof, as they occasionally do, are you prey to the pitch. And that, of course, is an even worse time than usual to invest in strategic metals.

Cash

Cash is variously meant to mean *cash*, as in dollar bills, or "cash equivalents"—things like money-market funds or

Treasury bills that you could immediately turn into cash, but that pay some interest until you do. To hold cash (of whichever variety) is to sit on the sidelines. This is sometimes the wisest, but most difficult, thing to do.

Tax Timing

It is common advice that you not let tax considerations interfere with investment decisions. Don't hang on to a stock to avoid paying tax on your gain if, by doing so, your gain will gradually disappear, or wait for a gain to go long term if it's likely to evaporate while you do.

Even so, there are a few things to keep in mind:

+ All your gains and losses for any given tax year get lumped together. Losses wipe out gains. If, as the year draws to a close, you have net gains, you may want to take enough losses to wipe them out and avoid having to pay tax. In fact, you might want to take extra losses, because up to $3,000 of net losses in any given year can be deducted from ordinary income. (Anything above $3,000 is carried over to future years.) If you're in the 33% tax bracket (between federal and state income tax), a $3,000 deduction saves you $1,000.

+ If you are in a high tax bracket, long-term gains are more valuable than short-term gains. Currently there is a 20% ceiling on the rate at which they can be taxed if held more than a year.* Thus—other things being equal—it's better to use losses to cancel out short-term gains (and thus save a heavy tax) than to cancel out long-

---

* For assets bought after passage of the 1997 law and held five years, the rate drops down to 18%. (For low-bracket taxpayers, the 20% and 18% rates are reduced to 10% and 8% respectively.) Congress will of course fiddle with all this from time to time, and even now there are exceptions: a higher 28% rate applies no matter how long you've held things like collectibles. And with a real estate gain, the portion that represents recapture of depreciation is taxed at 25%. All part of Congress's commitment to simplify the tax code.

term gains (and derive a somewhat less impressive tax benefit).

❖ If you bought a stock at 20 that's now 15, you might save taxes by selling it for a loss . . . but if it was a good buy at 20, might it be an even better value at 15? You don't want to get into the habit of buying high and selling low. There are three ways of dealing with this (if you calculate that your tax savings will justify the extra brokerage commissions): You could sell the stock to establish your loss, then buy it back 31 days later (the IRS disallows anything less as a "wash sale"). Or, if you have this unreasoning terror that the stock will take off during those intervening 31 days, as it could, you can do it the other way around. Buy a *second* 100 shares, wait 31 days, and then sell the *first* 100 for the loss. The hope is they won't fall further during the month you've doubled up. Or, if this 31-day notion throws you, sell your shares for a loss right now, but simultaneously buy something you consider similar—swap GM for Ford, say, or one AA-rated bond for another.

❖ Remember that if you make large gifts to charity, the best way to do it is usually by giving securities in which you have a long-term gain. You avoid paying *any* tax on the gain, yet get a deduction for the full value of the securities as of the date your charity receives them. (This emphatically does *not* work with short-term gains! You only get to deduct the *cost* of the gift, not its appreciated value.)

❖ None of this matters inside a tax-sheltered retirement account.

VSP

Sounds like an important brandy, but it's actually what you have to remember to tell your broker to identify *which* 50 shares of Intel you're selling. You have 200 shares, but they were bought piecemeal at different times. You may have a long-term profit on some of the shares and a short-term profit on the rest—or even a gain on some and a loss on others. If you're selling just 50 shares, it becomes important to know which 50 they are. You say they're the ones that provide you with a short-term loss, but why should the tax man trust you? He will assume the shares you've sold are the ones you've held longest. But what if that's not your intention? The way to handle this is to tell your broker to sell 50 Intel "versus purchase ten one ninety-two"— namely, the shares you bought October 1, 1992. Your broker, of course, doesn't care in the slightest which 50 shares you are selling, and he is hardly going to go running around for the right stock certificate, in part because no one seems to use stock certificates anymore. They use electronic ledger entries. But your confirm will arrive duly noted "VSP 10/1/92," and all will be square between you and the United States of America.

Re-org

I can't imagine you'll run into this. With luck, I'll never run into it again, either. But in the bowels of most brokerage firms dwells a department called "re-org." My conception of "re-org" is that it is made up of plainclothesmen whose extensions at the firm are unlisted.

I know about re-org because I once owned a stock that was converted through some exchange offer for bonds. It was not something I paid close attention to (this is why we have brokers, and why brokers have computers), but every month thereafter an entry appeared in my statement showing that I owned four GEICO bonds. After several months, I disposed of two of them. Several months later, the other two. No problem. More months passed. Then out of the blue came a call from my full-service broker. Re-org, he said, had just notified him they were debiting my account for $1,719. They said I had sold four GEICO bonds when in reality I had only owned two.

"Re-org?" I asked. I couldn't really make out what he was saying.

"Re-org," he said.

"Who the hell is re-org?" I asked.

"Re-org. They're down in the basement or something. I don't know."

"Well, how can they just take money out of my account? Don't I get to argue about it first?" I asked.

"I argued for you," he said. "You lost."

My broker, who as I've explained is by now a close friend, was genuinely upset by re-org's high-handed tactics—but helpless.

"But the four bonds were in my account for more than a year!" I said.

"I know," he said. "Apparently there should only have been two." He recited a litany of conversion ratios and transfers and journal entries that re-org had supplied to substantiate its case. And it seemed clear (in a hazy sort of way) that re-org was right. But a year later?

"You mean, they can make a mistake and confirm it in fourteen monthly statements and then, out of the blue, come and loot my account?" I asked.

"Yes," said my broker, "and they're going to debit you for the interest you were paid on the two extra bonds, plus interest on the proceeds of the second sale. They wanted you to pay the loss they're going to take to buy back the two extra bonds, because they've gone up since you sold them, but I put my foot down."

For weeks afterward I would call with outlandish pronouncements, delivered in my most dictatorial tone, in the name of re-org. "This is re-org," I would bellow. "We see here a dividend check that was not credited properly to the Tobias account in the fourth quarter of 1953. You shall credit his account at once—*at once,* do you hear me?—with 27 years' interest *und* penalties."

To date, re-org has not called to correct any year-old errors made accidentally in *its* favor.

Internet Investing

Investing via the Internet has come into its own. This has led some people to cut their trading costs dramatically—trades that only recently would have cost $125 or $250 in commissions can now cost less than $10. *Nothing,* for all practical purposes. What's more, the Internet has allowed many of those same people to all but close the gap between the kind of information they can get—and when they get it—versus "the professionals."

Thus for the right kind of person—the disciplined investor who does his homework—Internet investing is a boon. Why pay some fund 1.5% a year in management fees and expenses when you could just do it yourself? *And* control the tax consequences of your portfolio?*

But for every person you know who is disciplined, financially savvy, and does his homework, is it not fair to say you know twenty who aren't or don't? For no small percentage of them, Internet investing has become just one more way to gamble . . . an addiction. It's likely to wreck more than a few marriages and even a few lives. No doubt it already has.

---

* This tax issue is worth considering even with a low-expense index fund. Buying an index fund is great. But what if you had $90,000 and the patience simply to put it into the 30 Dow stocks yourself, at $3,000 a pop? The Dow may not be the best index to use, but it's the one everybody watches and, for the purposes of this exercise, has the virtue of containing only 30 stocks. Your total cost, if you used one of those $8-a-trade Internet brokers, would be $240. With no ongoing two-tenths-of-a-percent management fee, you'd save $180 a year. Alone, that wouldn't be worth it. (Who wants to get 30 quarterly reports in the mail every 90 days, 30 proxy statements each year?) But here's the big advantage: say two years have passed and the Dow is up 10%. Nothing much. But within the 30 stocks, one of them is up 80% and one is down 50%. You could sell the loser and get a tax benefit . . . buying it back 31 days later to reestablish your position (the IRS will disallow your tax loss as a "wash sale" if you have bought the same shares within 30 days before or after the sale) . . . use the winner to do the charitable giving you had planned to do with cash, buying *it* back moments later. Life may be too short to go to all this effort. Still, the option of managing the tax consequences of your portfolio is an advantage you don't get with a mutual fund—even an index fund.

"My name's Alan," begins a TV commercial you may have seen, with the speaker addressing a group of his peers, "and I haven't used . . . [long pause, as you are expecting him to say alcohol or cocaine] . . . E*Trade . . . since yesterday." "Hi, Alan!" responds the crowd (or maybe I just imagine that part), and the commercial goes on to say that Alan is building up his nest egg via this popular Internet broker. He may indeed be able to build it up a lot faster via an Internet broker than the old-fashioned, high-commission way. Absolutely. I've cut my own commissions 90% versus the trades I still do (out of loyalty, mainly) with my traditional broker. But I also think the Internet will lead many a lamb to slaughter. It's so easy to click "OK" a few times and make a $10,000 bet. Look how mesmerized we become on a stool in front of a slot machine. Internet investing positively *teases* you to play. It makes you feel powerful—moving thousands of dollars in and out, click, click, click. Talk about computer games!

But click often enough—even just once or twice a week—and four things will surely get you: the commissions (they're low, but imagine a slot machine that charged $5 or $10 a crank), the spreads (another $25, typically, on a 200 share trade), the taxes (a big chunk of your winnings, versus a much smaller chunk, deferred, if you buy and hold), and human nature. There are few places where one's self-destructive tendencies are more likely to surface than in an addictive gambling situation.

Thus for many investors, despite the allure of the game, index funds really do remain the smart way to play.

The Only Other Investment Guides You Might Want to Read

As I said in Chapter 1, even if this is the only investment guide you'll ever need, it is hardly the only one that's any good. To get an idea of how difficult it is to beat the market, and for a very readable tour: *A Random Walk Down Wall Street* by Burton Malkiel. For a different slant: *One Up on*

Wall Street by Peter Lynch and John Rothchild or *Buffett: The Making of an American Capitalist* by Roger Lowenstein.

But remember, the more time you spend reading about the stock market, the more you are likely to want to try your hand. Are you sure you want to begin devoting a good portion of your waking, worrying life in pursuit of this hobby? Have you the temperament to succeed? Can you afford to lose? Are you really that likely to outdo the pros in your spare time? Have you made out well with past sorties into the market?*

If not, then just buy—and hold—a few no-load mutual funds.

---

* The aforementioned ladies-only investment club in Beardstown, Illinois, received an enormous amount of publicity for earning returns averaging 23.4% per year for the first decade of their club's existence. It turned out that the rate of return had actually been only 9.1% per year, at a time the market was growing at 15.3%. The ladies would have been far better off just putting their money into an index fund, though their books would have been less fun.

Another widely circulated idea was that the average person could significantly outperform the market averages just by buying the ten highest-yielding stocks in the Dow each year. Refinements were developed to improve the return even more. In reality, this strategy only worked so well during the time period *before* the book first recommending it was published, and the author himself stopped using it in 1993. But the book advising this strategy continued to sell well for years after. Again, index funds would have made better investments.

(I, too, would probably have been better off leaving my money in index funds over the past 30 years, but I consider it my obligation to make all manner of crazy investments to test them out for *you*.)

CHAPTER **10**

What to Do If You Inherit a Million Dollars; What to Do Otherwise

If I had put just two million dollars *into that deal, I'd be a rich man today!*

—A REAL ESTATE MAN WE KNOW
(back in the days when $2 million was a lot of money)

As television viewers of the fifties all know, coming into a million dollars, even if it is tax-free, is not all applause and confetti. In fact, it can cause all kinds of inner demons to surface.

Listen to Gail Sheehy, author of the huge best-seller *Passages*. Did coming into money cause her any problems?

"Yeees!" she cries plaintively. "It makes me sweat a lot more, it makes me embarrassed and guilty—I mean, truly, it's terrible.

"It's much more fun being the aspirant, because once you have gotten there, even if you are just there temporarily (as you must continually remind yourself you are), you're in a position of defending or protecting rather than aspiring or building.

"It's terribly uncomfortable. It's also a problem that is *totally* unsympathetic to anyone who has five cents less than you do. Right? So there's nobody you can talk to."

When it first became clear that *Passages* had hit the jackpot, Sheehy was chatting with Random House editor Jason Epstein. Said he: "Yes, well. Money. You will find, Gail dear, that it will now be a dull ache in the back of your head. *Forever*."

"It was so ominous," Gail says, "and it was exactly how I felt!"

Sheehy has been rich and Sheehy has been, if not poor, nearly so. "I can't say that I was happiest when I was living in a fourth-floor walk-up on East Seventh Street with a one-year-old baby, you know, carting her on one hip and the wash on the other when I came home from work." But neither is she now laughing all the way to the bank.

Many of us, needless to say, would have an easier time than Gail Sheehy "coping" with a fast million or two. Or think we would. Or would love at least the chance to try.

Still, the problem with sudden wealth seems less how to invest it than how to keep it from wrecking your life. You will notice that in movies and novels where the hero actually manages to pull it off—to steal, win, or discover a fortune—they always end the action there. As if to say that the happiness with which they lived ever after goes without saying. When, in fact, the real story is that the screenwriter or novelist knows full well that this is not true, and can't think of a thing to write that wouldn't be anticlimactic.

Sheehy, with great good sense, has tried hard to avoid what she calls "that classic American trap—which is, you suddenly get a windfall and then, instead of living pretty much as you have, only a little better and with lots more security behind you—with money there to do something amazing every once in a while when it really counts—you suddenly leap up to meet that income level and always bubble up over it, and then are constantly running to keep up with this tremendous overhead you've established." It is a financial equivalent to the Peter Principle—getting yourself in, no matter how much you have, just a little too deep for comfort.

What to do, then, should you have the ill fortune to inherit a million dollars? Or, worse still, two?*

1. Go out for a very nice dinner.

2. Put about one year of normal living expenses someplace liquid, like a bank or money-market fund.

3. Put roughly equal sums into U.S. Treasury securities maturing in one, two, three, and four years.

4. Put the bulk of the remaining money into stock-index funds, split between domestic and foreign investments.

5. Buy a country place or a bigger house, if you want one—but not so big that the cost of carrying it will in any way strain you.

   5a. If you have the inclination and can find a good value, buy a small rental property, too. It will provide an inflation hedge and a little tax shelter.

   5b. *Do not buy a boat.*

6. Put, at most, 5% into silver—bags of silver dimes minted back in the days when they really were silver— keeping most of it in a bank vault and one bag in a very good hiding place at home. (Call Investment Rarities, 800-328-1860, for a quote.) This is your rich person's disaster hedge—a form of insurance. Don't expect it to be a good investment. But if inflation hits with a vengeance, silver could do even better than gold. Historically, silver has risen 11% for every 1% increase in inflation, versus 6% for gold. And in the event of a calamity, it may be easier to buy a loaf of bread with an old silver dime than with a by-then $6,000 gold coin.

---

* "A million" actually doesn't mean quite what it did in 1978. The equivalent today would be about $2.5 million—or $5 million if you want equivalency with *The Millionaire,* where John Beresford Tipton gave it away each week so you could sit back and watch it (in black and white) wreck someone's life. Yet the term "millionaire" will die hard, even if it now really means "five-millionaire" or "twenty-five millionaire." You could find a single million stretched thin with the list that follows. But do the best you can.

7. Be sure your will is in order.

8. Now, relax and forget the whole thing. Review it once a year, mainly to roll over your Treasury securities as they come due. Don't spend any of the investment principal, but enjoy the extra income it throws off.

If even this seems too hard, just choose a no-load mutual fund family and split your windfall a third, a third, a third among a broadly diversified U.S. stock fund, a broadly diversified international fund, and a money-market fund. Draw from the money fund when you feel like it and re-balance the three accounts once a year. (That is, if your international stocks now represent 40% of the pie, because they've grown fastest, shift some of the gain into the other two slices, so they remain about a third, a third, and a third.) You can probably take out about 4% a year and still have the rest grow enough to keep up with inflation. But if you spend a little more once in a while, so what?

This is not the way to get every last dollar from your inheritance—but isn't not-having-to-try one of the luxuries being a millionaire should bring?

Unless you want to switch from being whatever you were being to being a financier; unless you enjoy worrying about money and taking risks and paying taxes on profits and stewing over your losses; unless you are intrigued by the machinations of the Fed's Open Market Committee and the effects on the financial markets of the latest fiduciary fad—you should simply structure your assets, should you be so fortunate as to have them in such abundance, so as to give you security and peace of mind.

Life is not a business, as my father used to say. Why not set yourself up comfortably and stop worrying?

That's what *I* plan to do when the man from the contest-judging organization calls up to tell me that, by placing my YES! token in the "No, I don't wish to purchase any of these magazines but would like to enter the sweepstakes anyway" slot, I've won first prize.

Now what to do in the meantime.

Mutual Funds

Far more practical for most investors than trying to go it alone in the stock market—which is at the very least time-consuming, and possibly a good deal worse for the financially suicidal among us—is the no-load, low-expense mutual fund.

Admittedly, for many investors profits are only part of the objective. Much of the reward is the fun—challenge—intrigue—of the game itself. I am an investor, and I am the first to admit it. But that's not called investing, strictly speaking. It's called playing.

"The prudent way is also the easy way," counsels Paul Samuelson, nationally renowned economist, in a column he wrote for *Newsweek*. Someone else does the research, someone else does the worrying, someone else holds your certificates and provides a record of your dividends and capital gains for tax purposes. "What you lose is the daydream of that one big killing. What you gain is sleep."

Mutual funds provide wide diversification. Most allow you to have small amounts of money transferred from your checking account each month, so you can make steady investments automatically. Most are also geared to set up Keogh and IRA accounts with a minimum of paperwork and expense. Many are part of "fund families" like Fidelity or Vanguard that allow you to switch your money from one to another—from their aggressive-growth stock fund to their tax-exempt bond fund, for example—as often as you like. Just pick up the phone.

With mutual funds, the risks of the stock market are still there. Many funds declined 60% and more after the speculative binge of the late sixties and/or in 1973–74. But at least you don't have to make all the foolish decisions yourself. You need only decide which funds to invest in, how much, and when. In this very real sense, you are still managing your own money.

Indeed, they offer you the chance to make another money management call: mutual funds make it practical for you to diversify *globally*. And while many people consider investing abroad dangerous, international diversification can actually *reduce* your risk. Stock markets of different countries move up and down at least somewhat independent of each other. A U.S. investor in 1929 who was wise enough to place 50% in foreign stocks would have needed only five years to recover from the worst crash in American history. A Japanese investor in 1990 who had 50% of his money outside of Japan—likewise. At the same time as it reduces risk, international diversification can actually boost returns—especially if the U.S. stock market ever tires of its almost continuous bull market since 1982. The rest of the world has discovered capitalism in a big way, and there is no reason that you shouldn't try to capitalize on that while reducing your exposure to the dangers of a bear market here.

The first step in choosing among mutual funds is about the only one that is at all clear-cut. There are funds that charge initial sales fees of as much as 8.5%, known as the "load"; and there are others that charge no load. *Choose a no-load fund.* Or *certainly* no fund that charges more than a 2% or 3% load. To do otherwise is to throw money out the window.*

Statistical studies show that no-load funds perform just as well (and as badly) as load funds. This stands to reason, because the load goes not toward superior management of the fund, but to the salesmen who sell it. And they have no influence over its performance. Yet most people still buy load funds. As long as there are people out selling, there will be people in buying. Don't be one of them.

(If you already own shares in a load fund, the load alone is no reason to sell—you've already paid it. But neither is it a reason not to sell. What's lost is lost.)

---

* An 8.5% load is even worse than it sounds. When you send $1,000 to such a fund, you give up $85 in commissions, so that you are really paying $85 to invest $915—fully 9.3%. A more typical 5.75% load works out to 6.1%.

Sure, there have been some unbelievably successful load funds, such as Fidelity's famed Magellan Fund. But so, too, have there been unbelievably successful no-loads. A dollar invested in the Twentieth Century Growth fund when it was founded in 1958 is worth around $200 today.

In choosing a no-load fund, there are several things to consider. Two things to look at, of course, are the management fees and the administrative expenses: These annual charges can total less than half a percent or climb to as much as 3% or more. You have to have a very good reason to go with a fund that charges you more than 1% a year for its management and administration. (Many funds will advertise their low management fee without mentioning the other annual expenses and "12b-1" marketing fees they charge. Be sure to dig for the total fees and expenses before investing.)

What really matters, of course, is not what a fund will charge you, but what it will *earn* for you. Here you can be much less certain.

Tracked over several up and down cycles in the stock market and graded from A to F on the basis of their relative performance, many funds will rank A or B in bull markets—but D or F in bad ones. This is not because the managers are brilliant some years and dunces in others, but rather because these funds have highly volatile ("high-beta") stocks in their portfolios. Other funds, the less volatile ones, are most likely to rank C or D in up markets, as their stocks climb in the "slow lane" relative to the others, but B or A in bad markets, when they merely slip while others slide, tumble, and plunge.

You can see, then, how dangerous it is to choose a fund based on its recent past performance, as many people do. They may buy a fund that has performed even better than the bull market—at the very time that the bull market is petering out and the fund is shifting from its A rating to its F rating.

If you knew which way the market were headed at any

given time, it would be a simple matter of buying the highly volatile funds at the depths of a bear market, just as things were about to turn, and then switching to the conservative funds (or getting out of the market altogether) just as things were peaking.

However, if you do not have this happy facility—and who does?—then what you are looking for is that rare mutual fund that does better than average in both up *and* down markets, as few do. Several of these I have listed in the appendix "Selected Mutual Funds" (page 222), although it must be stressed that *past performance is no guarantee of future performance.* Who is to say that the money manager most responsible for a fund's success in a given two- or three-year period is even still at his desk? *People* manage money, after all, not "funds"—and people move on to new and better jobs, or retire.

If you have mutual-fund paralysis, just buy shares in one of Vanguard's index funds (800-662-7447). Their hallmark is keeping expenses low, which means almost all your money goes to work for you. Over the long run, your performance will just about match that of the stock market as a whole—which is better than most mutual funds do, because most burden your investment with higher management fees. **This is a very simple concept but profound: just by investing all the money you have earmarked for the stock market in the Vanguard Index Trust, you will generally do better than most bank trust departments, mutual fund managers, and private investors—with far less effort!**

One more advantage of index funds is that they do little trading. As a result, they generate few taxable gains. You have to pay tax on the dividends they earn each year, but most of the *growth* is tax-free until you sell the shares. That means "the government's" share of your money continues to work for you, and earn dividends, until you sell the fund. This doesn't matter within the shelter of a retirement plan, but it certainly makes a difference for unsheltered money.

Closed-end Funds

One kind of no-load mutual fund that particularly bears consideration is the "closed-end" fund. Such funds originally sold a set number of shares to the public, raising, say, $100 million to invest. Then they closed the doors to new money. Investors who wished to cash in their shares would sell them just as they would sell any regular stock, through any broker, to some other investor. Presumably, if the fund managers had turned the $100 million into $120 million, each share in the fund would be worth 20% more than it was at the outset. Or so everyone assumed. But things are only worth what people will pay for them, and shares in closed-end funds sank to discounts that ranged from a few percentage points up to 30% and more. (A few funds rose to premiums.) As I write this, for example, you can buy a dollar's worth of assets in the Mexico Fund for 76 cents or the Templeton Dragon Fund for 84 cents. Or a dollar's worth of assets in the Morgan Stanley Africa Investment Fund for 78 cents or its Asia-Pacific Fund for 82 cents. (There are lots of closed-ends that invest in U.S. securities, too.) This won't do you much good if the managers of those funds have picked a dreadful assortment of stocks that all collapse—but it's just about as hard to pick bad stocks as good, so that is unlikely. More likely, you will have a dollar working for you even though you only had to pay 75 or 85 cents.

The risk is that the discount, irrational to begin with, could widen still further by the time you went to sell your shares. On the other hand, the discount could narrow—which at least makes more sense, even if it's not necessarily more likely to happen.

There's actually a sound reason for closed-ends to trade at a discount. They're burdened by a handicap: namely, the 1% or more in management and administrative fees many subtract each year. If the stocks in the fund grew by 10% a year including dividends, the net asset value of the fund itself would grow at only 9%, after expenses. (Of course, that's true of open-end funds, too, and you can never get *them* at a discount.) Closed-ends may also trade at a well-deserved discount if their managers have demonstrated a consistent talent for making poor investments.

Then again, closed-ends offer two conceptual advantages over open-end funds. First, when trading at a substantial discount, a closed-end is like a *less-than-no-load* fund. You get $1 worth of assets working for you for 80 cents. Second, closed-end fund managers need not worry that, in a down market, they will be flooded with redemptions, forcing them to keep cash idle to redeem shares—or to dump holdings at what may be exactly the wrong time. So they may be able to do a better job managing the fund. True, they don't have the same incentive as with open-end funds. (With an open-end fund, good performance draws new investors, swelling the management fee; poor performance leads to redemptions and lower fees.) But they still have an incentive, because increasing the value of the fund also increases the management fee. And there is the ego factor—particularly now that "personality" closed-ends, like the Zweig and Gabelli funds, have appeared on the market along with the faceless institutional funds.

Ask a broker for more information on closed-end funds, which trade just like stocks. *Barron's* and Monday's *Wall Street Journal* carry quotations for these "Publicly Traded Funds" in a separate box in the financial section, including the discount at which each sells.

❖ Never buy a closed-end fund when it is first issued (because sales charges will be built into the price and it will likely fall to a discount).

❖ Rarely buy a closed-end fund at a premium (because then you're paying $1.05 or $1.30 to get $1 working for you), unless you're really convinced that the manager is so good he can beat the averages by enough to overcome both the drag of his management fee and the extra drag of having to make $1 do the work of $1.05 or $1.30.

Spiders, Diamonds, and WEBS

There are closed-end funds that operate like index funds, and at an even slightly lower expense fee. You can buy and sell them just like stocks. Spiders, as they're nicknamed (Standard & Poors Depository Receipts), follow the S&P 500 index and trade on the American Stock Exchange with the symbol SPY. Diamonds (symbol DIA) also trade on the Amex and give you the Dow Jones industrial average. Both are geared to avoid selling at a premium or discount, so they really are very much like open-ended index funds.* You should choose whichever is more convenient. Spiders and Diamonds are good if you tend to buy stocks directly through a deep-discounter. Index funds make more sense if you are basically a mutual fund investor and already have your money with Vanguard or Fidelity or one of the other companies with a very low expense index fund.

WEBS are "world equity benchmark shares," and work the same way, only for the stock markets of other countries. There are WEBS for Japan—symbol EWJ—Belgium— EWK—and well over a dozen more, but they are less obviously a great deal. That's because, at least as of this writing, the annual expenses they charge are often close to what actively managed foreign funds might charge. And overseas, active management may give you more of an edge than it does in America, where the markets tend to be well regulated, relatively efficient, and thus hard to beat. Remember: no one said active management was, per se, a bad thing; just that in the investment horse race, the fund with the 20-pound jockey is likely, over time, to beat those with the 150-pound jockeys. Well, if *both* jockeys weigh 150 pounds, it doesn't hurt to have the one with a brain.

---

* One twist: you can short them. But over the long run, one would have gone very broke shorting the American stock market.

The Future

What you should do with your money naturally depends on what the future holds.

If inflation accelerates, interest rates will rise and bonds will fall. Most stocks will probably fall, too. If you anticipate accelerating inflation, you want to avoid fixed-income securities.

If you anticipate a classic depression—I don't—then you want to buy long-term Treasury bonds. In a classic depression, interest rates will fall to near zero, and you will have what everybody wants: something completely safe that yields (as I write this) nearly 6% a year.

The conventional wisdom among best-selling financial writers of the seventies and eighties was that we would have some of each. Unemployment and recession would get so bad that the fiscal and monetary floodgates would be thrown open to avert depression, bringing on inflation even worse than the last bout. To fight it, the Fed would slam on the brakes—they have to slam harder and harder each time to have any impact—and throw the country into an even greater slump. Around and around it would go, inflation, recession, inflation, recession, getting worse and worse. The "malarial economy," Howard Ruff and others dubbed it—alternating chills and fever and, eventually, collapse. Ruff wrote *How to Profit from the Coming Bad Years* and (when they didn't come) *How to Survive and Win in the Inflationary Eighties* (which proved to be highly disinflationary). Douglas Casey cashed in with *Crisis Investing*. Ravi Batra hit #1 with *The Great Depression of 1990*. James Dale Davidson and William Rees-Mogg weighed in with *The Great Reckoning: Protect Yourself in the Coming Depression*, followed by *Blood in the Streets: Investment Profits in a World Gone Mad*.

And so it went.

"But there is another scenario which should not be dismissed out of hand," I wrote in this space in 1983, "unaccustomed though we've become to improvement: That this decade, if we keep our wits about us, could become what Paul Volcker has called the mirror image of the last one: falling energy prices, falling inflation, falling interest rates, rising productivity, rising real wages, rising employment. I make no secret of being partial to the optimistic scenario. I think we've laid a technological base that places us, potentially at least, on the brink of unparalleled prosperity."

I still believe that.

The catch is that—with the U.S. stock market up 12-fold since 1983—one should not expect nearly the same kinds of returns over the next 15 years.

Sermonette

Whether you choose mutual funds or a direct plunge into the stock market, bonds, or a savings account; whether you shelter your investments through a Keogh Plan or an IRA; and whether you spend now or save to spend later—you will find that, by the prevailing American ethic, anyway, you never have enough.

D. H. Lawrence wrote a wonderful story years ago called "The Rocking-Horse Winner." "Although they lived in style," Lawrence wrote of his fictional family, "they felt always an anxiety in the house. . . . There was always the grinding sense of the shortage of money, though the style was always kept up. . . . And so the house came to be haunted by the unspoken phrase: *There must be more money! There must be more money!* The children could hear it all the time, though nobody said it aloud. They could hear it at Christmas, when the expensive and splendid toys filled the nursery. Behind the shining modern rocking horse, behind the smart doll's house, a voice would start whispering: 'There *must* be more money! There *must* be more money!' "

One of the children began playing the horses. Before long, in league with the gardener, he had managed to turn a few pennies into a small fortune. The child arranged to have it given to his mother, anonymously. "Then something very curious happened. The voices in the house suddenly went mad, like a chorus of frogs on a spring evening." Debts were paid off and new luxuries lavished—"and yet the voices . . . simply trilled and screamed in a sort of ecstasy: 'There must be more money! Oh-h-h; there must be more money. Oh, now, now-w! Now-w-w—there must be more money!—more than ever! More than ever!'"

More is never enough. But there may be a way around this for some people, a way to be just as contented and happy if you don't inherit a million dollars as if you do. It is suggested by this passage from *Stone Age Economics* by Marshall Sahlins:

> By the common understanding, an affluent society is one in which all the people's material wants are easily satisfied. . . . [But] there are two possible courses to affluence. Wants may be "easily satisfied" either by producing much or desiring little. The familiar conception, the Galbraithean way, makes assumptions peculiarly appropriate to market economics: that man's wants are great, not to say infinite, whereas his means are limited, although improvable: thus, the gap between means and ends can be narrowed by industrial productivity. . . . But there is also a Zen road to affluence, departing from premises somewhat different from our own: that human material wants are finite and few, and technical means unchanging but on the whole adequate. Adopting the Zen strategy, a people can enjoy an unparalleled material plenty—with a low standard of living.

Or as a friend of mine once said: "It's just as easy to live well when you're poor as when you're rich—but when you're poor, it's much cheaper."

This is not to advocate Buddhism, asceticism, Spartanism—or, for that matter, poverty. I, for one, like living a little better every year. In fact, I believe happiness lies less in how much you have than in which way you're headed. Which is a strong argument for saving something each year rather than see your net worth slip backward; and for *pacing* your acquisition of the finer things, lest the day come when you can't afford them. For remember: a luxury once sampled becomes a necessity. It's not so bad living on a low floor—until you've had a view.

Ultimately, how you should spend or invest your money depends not so much on price-earnings ratios or dividend rates as on those larger questions that forever lurk, but generally go unasked: Who am I? What am I trying to do with my life? Is money the means or the end?

There is a good measure of self-knowledge required to choose the proper investment course. It has even been postulated that many small investors in the stock market, without knowing it, secretly want to lose. They jump in with high hopes—but feeling vaguely guilty. Guilty over "gambling" with the family's money, guilty over trying to "get something for nothing," or guilty over plunging in without really having done much research or analysis. Then they punish themselves, for these or other sins, by selling out, demoralized, at a loss.

In any event, whether or not they secretly want to, many investors, failing to seek out value and then hold it patiently, do lose. If this little book saved you $1,000 a year—on wine (by the case, on sale), on life insurance and finance charges, on brokerage commissions (trading less often, and with a deep-discount broker), on investment letters (not subscribing to them) and on taxes (particularly with a Keogh Plan or IRA)—I would be delighted. But if it saved you from getting burned in the stock market, or on even one seemingly surefire "investment" someone was trying to sell you—I would be thrilled!

(I hear, by the way, that the Mexican peso is now very strong again, and that you can get a hell of an interest rate south of the border.)

Appendixes

"I have no idea how much my interest rate is," says Suzanne Carver, a Chicago housewife, as she paws through her purse to check her card. "It doesn't say on here. Well, as long as I can buy things with it, who cares?"

—*The Wall Street Journal,*
March 19, 1987

Earning 177% on Bordeaux

This example has sort of evolved. The first time I used it was in 1978, on the *Tonight Show*. Say you bought a $10 bottle of wine for dinner every Saturday night, but could instead get a 10% discount buying by the case. You'd "make" 10% on the extra money you tied up. And you'd "make" it in just 12 weeks—a bottle a week for 12 weeks equals one case of wine—which works out, I explained, to "better than a 40% annual return."

I didn't explain how *much* better. I figured 40% was dramatic enough. Where else can you earn 40% tax-free?

As the years passed, I found people were having trouble understanding this little shtick of mine. Why is it 40% if I just got a 10% discount?

So I tried explaining it in a little more detail. What actually happens, I explained, is that instead of going to the store and laying out $10 for one bottle, you are laying out $108 for 12 bottles—$120 less the 10% discount. Which means you are laying out $98 more than you otherwise would have. That extra $98 is your "investment." By keeping at most that much extra tied up all year, you save $1 a week on wine—$52 a year. And "earning" $52 a year by tying up $98 is earning 53%.

So now I was up to 53%, an even better tax-free return.

This confused people even more. That first $98 is gone, they would tell me, and now you have to come up with a new $98 to buy your next case of wine.

But think about it. If you were someone who planned to spend $10 every week on wine—$520 a year—and who would have LOVED to save 10% buying by the case but just couldn't scrape up enough money all at once to do it, how much financing would you need?

Would you have to go to a bank and ask for a $400 line of credit in order to be able to change your buying habits?

No, you would need only a $98 credit line—and you would only fully draw it down that very first week. After that, you would replenish it by $10 a week (the $10 you used to spend on wine by the bottle), which means that after 12 weeks, when you needed to buy the next case, you would not only have replenished the full $98, you'd actually have an extra $12 to work with (the money you saved buying by the case). So now you'd have to draw down only $86 of your $98 credit line.

In other words, to finance this change in habits you'd need a maximum credit line of $98. But you'd only actually draw down that much the very first week. Within 10 weeks you'd have paid the balance down to zero; then run it back up to $86 in the 13th week to buy your next case of wine; then paid that off in 9 weeks; then run it back up to $74 to buy your *next* case—and so on. On average, over the course of the year, you're using far less than the full $98 to finance this change in buying habits.

So the return on your decision to tie up that $98 at first, and then gradually less, is actually much greater than 40% or 53%.

If my friend Less Antman has keyed all this into his Hewlett-Packard financial calculator right—and I've never known him to err—it works out to an annualized 177% rate of return (though try explaining THAT in 40 seconds on the *Tonight Show*).

It's still only $52 you're earning—$1 a week by getting the 10% discount. But applied to all your regular shopping, it can be the best "investment" in your portfolio.

Next step: find a vintage you like equally well that's $8 a bottle.

How Much Life Insurance
Do You Need?

If you're single with no dependents, you need little—to assist with burial expenses and, posthumously, pay off a few debts—or none. The great push to sell college students life insurance is not entirely unlike the selling of ice to Eskimos, except that a lot more insurance is sold that way than ice.

If you're married, with a hopelessly incompetent spouse, a family history of heart disease, and a horde of little children, you should carry a great deal of insurance. Less if your spouse has a reliable income. Less still if you have fewer children or if those children have wealthy and benevolent grandparents. And still less as those children grow up.

If you are very rich, you need no insurance at all, except as it is helpful in providing liquidity to settle your estate. If you *live* richly off a high income but own outright little more than a deck of credit cards and some cardigan sweaters, it will take a lot of insurance to keep from exposing your dependents to an altogether seamier side of life when you are gone.

What you want, ideally, is enough insurance, when combined with whatever other assets you may have, to pay for what are euphemistically called "final expenses"—deathbed medical expenses not covered by other insurance, funeral expenses, possible postmortem emergencies like an illness of the surviving spouse, payment of bills—and then enough in addition to replace the income you had been kicking into the family till. So that, financially, anyway, you will not be missed.

Of course, you don't have to replace all your income, just the after-tax portion you were actually taking home. And not even that much, because with you gone, there will be one fewer mouth to feed, one fewer theater ticket to buy. Not to mention the savings on the second car or commuting expenses, medical and dental expenses, gambling losses, the subscription to *Business Week,* life insurance premiums, gifts, charitable contributions, clothing, laundry, on-line computer services, shaving cream—and the cigarettes that did you in in the first place. Your surviving dependents will need perhaps 75% to 85% of your current take-home pay in order to live as well, or nearly as well, as they were before. So if you were earning $38,000 a year and taking home $30,000, your family might maintain roughly the same living standard on $22,500 to $25,000 a year.

To figure your life insurance needs, estimate what your heirs would need if you died this afternoon. Then do the same for your spouse and his or her needs. A typical calculation goes as follows:

1. Estimate how much your heirs would need to replace if you died. For most families, this number falls somewhere around 75% of your annual take-home pay. If you take home no pay, but merely do 80 hours a week of cooking, cleaning, day caring, and shopping, estimate the cost of your replacement.

2. Subtract the annual Social Security benefits your family could expect to receive. Exact benefits depend on how high your earnings had been while alive and when you entered the system. (Perversely, the widow of a 23-year-old gets more than the widow of a man who'd been paying into the system for decades.) See page 213 for a ballpark idea.

3. The difference—if there is a difference—is the annual income gap you'll want life insurance to make up. But for how long? This depends on the ages of your children and spouse, and whether you'd expect your spouse to remarry. Choose a time period from the table below and multiply the annual income gap by the figure on the right. The result is an amount of insurance that should

last the number of years you require, if invested sensibly, and keep up with inflation. For example, to provide an additional $10,000 for 25 years, you'd multiply $10,000 by 18—$180,000.

	Multiply by:*
5 years	4.7
10 years	9
15 years	12
20 years	15
25 years	18
30 years	20
50 years	26

4. Add a lump sum as a cushion for funeral expenses, grief-induced family illnesses, the payment of worrisome debts—at least half a year's salary and in no event less than $15,000.

Now you have a grand total of your insurance needs. But wait!

5. Subtract whatever assets you've amassed such as savings accounts, stocks, bonds, and retirement accounts (including whatever pension benefits you'd be entitled to from work). Subtract still more if there's a wealthy and loving grandparent in the picture who would want to help out or whose wealth would eventually pass on to the family. And subtract the value of the group life insurance you have at work—but make a mental note that you may have to replace it if you switch jobs and that, in the event of a long terminal illness that forces you from your job, you will have to promptly exercise your

---

* This assumes your heirs could invest the proceeds to earn 3% after taxes and inflation. If you think they could earn more, you'd need less insurance— but you're probably not being realistic. The 3% assumption I've used may actually be optimistic.

(very expensive) option of continuing the policy on your own.

6. Round up to the nearest $25,000 or $50,000, and there's your answer. If it looks overwhelming, remember that you can stretch your coverage by purchasing term insurance instead of whole life, and by shopping for it carefully (see pages 24–25). Remember, too, that your spouse could remarry; your spouse could go to work; once the children are grown, *they* could provide support as well. Furthermore, it is not inconceivable that your family could be happy with a more modest lifestyle than they now enjoy.

How Much Social Security Will You Get?

A much-publicized 1994 poll found more young people believing in UFOs than in the possibility they would actually get anything back for all their Social Security contributions. This view is extreme but perhaps healthy—at least it means they're not counting on Uncle Sam to provide for their retirement.

When Social Security was launched in the thirties, there were forty people working for each person receiving benefits. But then something awkward happened. People started living longer. And having fewer kids. Today there are only three people working for each retiree. As the Baby Boomers begin to retire, it will approach two. At the same time, Congress kept upping the benefits.

With payroll taxes already sky-high, something's got to give. Two things, actually: the age at which you can retire with full Social Security benefits will be pushed back (already it's slated to rise from 65 to 67 gradually, beginning in 2003), and the amount you get to keep will shrink unless you really need the money.

Having the full-benefits age continue to rise past 67 (and perhaps having it reach 67 sooner than 2027 as currently planned) would go a long way toward assuring benefits to really old people—the growing millions in their eighties and nineties and beyond, who, if they failed to provide adequately for their own retirement, simply could not support themselves. It's also politically the most palatable change, because it doesn't affect anyone for a long time.

Squeezing the benefits will be less palatable but equally necessary. Social Security was never intended to be a full retirement plan. It was meant as a safety net for those who, through bad luck or poor planning—or the good fortune of living unusually long—had not saved enough to provide for themselves. It was meant to keep elderly people from starving, not to provide a 1990s' middle-class lifestyle. And until 1966, when Medicare was added to the system, it provided no health benefits.

Congress's generosity in periodically beefing up the benefits was great for getting votes. But in many it built the expectation that, having paid Social Security taxes, they were entitled to a nice retirement, courtesy of Uncle Sam. Few retirees today have any idea what a good deal they've got. In fact, most people believe that today's retirees, by and large, are getting back less than they paid into the system. But that's just never been true.

The very first Social Security check, for $22.54, was paid in 1940 to a Vermont woman who had paid $22 in Social Security taxes. By the time she died, in 1974, aged 100, she had collected $20,944.42. An extreme example, but the truth is that the average person retiring today at 65 gets back all the money he or she paid into Social Security, with interest, by age 71 or 72. "After that," Paul Hewitt, a budget expert at the National Taxpayers Union, told *Time,* "you're on welfare."

According to the Congressional Research Service, the average person who retired in 1980 got back all he—and his employer—paid into Social Security (including an adjustment for interest!) in under three years.

So the hard fact for today's older folks to accept is that, meager as Social Security benefits may seem, they are actually a very good deal.

The popular notion is to privatize Social Security. Have everyone save for themselves, and they'll do better. And we will doubtless move at least somewhat closer to that sort of scheme—more reliance on IRAs, less on Social Security checks. But it has two huge problems. First, what do you do for old folks who failed to invest wisely? Or who lived longer than average? (No need for *everyone* to save enough to last to age 103; but what if *you* live that long?) Are you going to let them starve in the street? Second, how do we get from here to there? It's fine for today's workers to say, "Just stop withholding FICA from my pay and I'll provide for myself!" But who will then provide for all the millions of elderly Americans who currently subsist on Social Security?

The long and the short of it is that—whatever it may be called by the time you retire—there is almost sure to be some sort of Social Security safety net. But the benefits it pays, especially to those who don't need them, are likely to be even less rich than today. So no matter what, you're wise to be thinking about this, and to put all you can—starting now!—into your IRA, your Keogh Plan, your profit-sharing plan at work, and, on top of that, into two or three carefully selected no-load, low-expense, stock-market mutual funds.

Having said all that, you can probably get a rough idea of the benefits you're entitled to by looking to see what they would be now, were you to retire, die, or become disabled today. In real dollars, real buying power, it's a sure bet the payments will not increase (how could we afford it?) nor decrease sharply (how could Congress allow it?).

Social Security benefits are tied to how much you have paid in to the system. What's more, in the case of death benefits, the payout to your surviving spouse will depend in part on your age at death and on the composition of your family. Therefore the examples shown here are to be taken as only the roughest guideline of what you might expect.

Examples of Annual Social Security Benefits Today

Recipient	Average	High
Worker retiring at 65, no dependents	$10,500	$15,000
Worker retiring at 65, with spouse	16,500	23,000
Disabled worker, no dependents	8,500	17,500
Disabled worker with dependents	14,000	26,000
Widow or widower at 65	8,500	16,000
Widow/er, caring for two or more kids	17,000	32,000

The figures assume, at the low end, an average payout and, at the high end, someone who consistently exceeded the maximum on which Social Security tax was levied. As recently as 1965, that ceiling was $4,800. By 1998, it had reached $68,400.

To qualify for benefits, no one needs credit for more than ten years of work covered by Social Security. The length of credit required ranges down to as little as 1½ years for people who become disabled or die in their early twenties.

If you are within several years of retirement, don't rely on the rough guidelines above. Write or call any of the 1,300 Social Security offices around the country and ask for the booklet and forms that will help you make a closer estimate.

A Few Words about Our National Debt

First, the bad news. The day Washington began slapping itself on the back for balancing the budget, we were still running a deficit well in excess of $100 billion. That's because of how we account for the Social Security Trust Fund and scores of other, much smaller, trust funds. *The surplus Social Security taxes we're supposed to be piling up for our old age are actually counted as "revenue" by Uncle Sam.* We're spending, not saving, it. In 1998, the Social Security surplus is expected to be around $100 billion. So whenever you hear a federal budget number, just subtract $100 billion. If you hear that the budget's balanced, then you'll know we're running a $100 billion deficit. A $50 billion surplus? No, a $50 billion *deficit.*

Imagine your own household budget. You spend $1,000 a week. You take in $940—plus $60 that your daughter gives you every week for safekeeping. She's saving up for college. Would you say your budget is balanced? You take in $1,000 a week, spend $1,000 a week. Yet, clearly, you are running a $60-a-week deficit, embezzling $60 a week from your daughter. About $3,000 a year. The day will come that your daughter presents you with the bill for Dartmouth and expects you to pay it with all that money she earned mowing lawns, sitting babies, designing websites.

In Uncle Sam's case, it's not $3,000 but upwards of $100 billion (though still just 6% or so of annual revenues).

The further bit of bad news is that when we did achieve a balanced budget in 1998—which is to say a $100 billion deficit—we did it in a prosperous economy. Imagine how the deficit might swell in a recession.

So before you rush out to spend any surplus, please bear in mind—and tell all your friends—it's not a surplus at all.

Or is it?

Here's the good news. *Because of the way Uncle Sam accounts for what any ordinary business would term "capital spending," things may not be nearly as bad as they seem.*

When a business buys a machine or a county builds a road, it amortizes the cost over the life of that machine or road. (I'm oversimplifying, but this is the general idea.) When Uncle Sam buys a machine or pays much of the cost to build a road, it "expenses" the full amount then and there, just as if it were paying the phone bill.

So just as we're shortchanging our children by the way we account for the Social Security surplus—spending the money we should be saving—so are we shortchanging ourselves in *their* favor by treating as a current expense the cost of projects that will benefit them many years into the future.

(Imagine your own household budget again. If you "spent" $195,000 one year, much of it borrowed, to buy a house, yet earned only $60,000 that year, would you say you ran a huge deficit? Uncle Sam would.)

You will be forgiven for wondering why we don't just do the accounting properly. Why not exclude the Social Security surplus from the budget numbers? And why not charge to future years a sensible portion of the capital investments we're making, as any business would? Hello? Is anybody home?

The first part—excluding the trust fund surpluses from budget revenue—would be easy. But the second is tougher than you might imagine. Clearly, building a road or a bridge is an investment. But how about a tank or a fighter plane? Funds for education? Midnight basketball? All these are investments in our future. (The goal isn't the basketball game per se, but helping to steer kids down the path to productive citizenship, working and paying taxes, rather than the path that leads to crime and incarceration, *absorbing* taxes.) Yet where would it end? One can imagine Congress sorely tempted by the lure of this kind of accounting. Could all education expenditures be written off over 50 years rather than "expensed" all at once? You can just see the free-for-all.

So in an odd sort of way, our irresponsible Social Security accounting may be more or less balanced by our conservatism in expensing capital expenditures.

In a sense, one might argue, our accumulated national debt—the sum of all those annual budget deficits we've been running, now up to about $5.5 trillion—is like the long-term debt of a company that's been making investments in the future. At a bit under 70% of our Gross Domestic Product, it's higher than we'd like, but by no means insupportable. It's been higher, it's been lower.

Especially in prosperous times, we should lean against the wind to lower that 70% ratio. Gradually reducing it to the 30% or so it was before the Vietnam war would improve our fiscal health. But here's the thing many people miss: it is the relative size of the debt, not the actual dollar amount, that matters. A $100 million debt would swamp most small businesses but mean nothing to an enterprise like Intel. Our $5.5 trillion debt would swamp Germany or France, but is not the end of the world for us. It's that 70% ratio, not the $5.5 trillion, we need to focus on and reduce.

If—with honest accounting for the trust fund surpluses— we ran a $110 billion deficit this year, we would expand the national debt by 2%. But if at the same time the economy grew by 5%—say, 2% inflation and 3% real growth— then the national debt would actually have *shrunk* relative to the economy as a whole. Keep this up for 50 years—2% growth in the debt, 5% growth in the economy—and you have a $90 trillion economy and a $15 billion debt. At which point the debt, far from approaching 70% of the Gross Domestic Product, would be not quite 17%.

This is not to deny the symbolic importance of a "balanced budget," however oddly it is calculated. But it does give one a somewhat more sanguine feeling about our fiscal affairs.

Less important than a zero deficit, let alone paying down the debt, is making the money that we do lay out count. Six hundred dollar hammers are obviously out; welfare payments to those who don't need them only breed dependency and cost self-esteem; unneeded pork barrel projects deserve the line-item veto.

In years of high tax revenues and low unemployment, we should be paying down the debt. But in most years, it's enough to have it grow slower than the economy as a whole.

Cocktail Party Financial Quips to Help You Feel Smug

1. If you are fully invested in the market (or wish to pretend you are), you can say: "I'm betting that the Fed will ease up." This means you think the Federal Reserve Board will ease up on interest rates, allowing them to fall and the stock market, as a consequence, to rise. Either this is the general consensus, in which case you will seem *au courant;* or it is a contrary opinion, in which case you will appear a shrewd man or woman of independent thought. No matter what "the Fed" is really doing, or how little you know of it or care, that you should have an opinion at all is impressive. If someone tries to pin you down, look genuinely uncomfortable—which won't be hard under the circumstances—and say, just a bit mysteriously: "Forgive me, I'd rather not discuss it just yet."

2. If you've cautiously avoided the stock market but someone asks you what you're into these days, you can say: "Gee, Bill, I really don't have much of a mind for stocks. I know I must be missing out on some terrific opportunities, but I'm happier just sticking to municipals." This will be taken as a display of false modesty—it will be assumed you really do have a mind for stocks—and it will indicate that you are a high-bracket taxpayer of considerable means. You will be envied.

3. Or: "I'll tell you the truth, Phil. I used to play the market until I toted up how much time I was spending on it— you know, the calls from my broker, downloading prices to update my portfolio, juggling the commodity straddles to save a few tax dollars. After the Dow hit 9300 in mid-'98, I took my profits and got out. I decided I'd rather spend the time with my kids." This is bound to make Phil feel guilty.

4. If someone is waxing philosophical about the market, you can say: "The great mistake made by the public is paying attention to prices instead of values." If that raises an eyebrow, because it sounds a bit more formal than you usually sound, you can continue: "Charlie Dow said that back at the turn of the century [which he did], and it's as true now as it was then [which it is]."

5. If someone is boasting about a stock that's really zoomed, you can say: "Gosh, that's terrific! Sounds like it's time to short some."

6. Or (if you're really fed up) you could say: "Gee, a regular Hetty Green!" Chances are, your companion will have no notion who Hetty Green was. ("The witch of Wall Street," she died in 1916, leaving $100 million to children who despised her.) But if his fists clench, suggesting that he somehow does know, flash a quick grin and say: "Just kidding, Phil. Just kidding."

Selected Discount Brokers

Commission schedules vary—find the one that best matches the kind of trading you do. Compare services also: Is margin available? At what rates? What discounts are available on options? How long are you kept waiting on "hold" on a busy day? Is there a local office for you to clap eyes on an actual human being (if you like that sort of thing) or will it all be done by phone and mail? What sort of touch-tone telephone trading is available? What sort of direct link to your computer? Will the firm hold your securities for you? Send you S&P sheets? Take orders and provide account information 24-hours-a-day? Allow you to write checks against the value of your securities? Wire money from your account upon request? Provide free stock quotes? Buy mutual funds for your account? For free?

Ameritrade   (800) 669-3900
Charles Schwab & Co   (800) 435-4000
E*Trade   (800) 786-2575
Fidelity Brokerage   (800) 544-8666
Kennedy Cabot   (800) 252-0090
Jack White   (800) 233-3411
Muriel Siebert   (800) 872-0444
National Discount Brokers   (800) 417-7423
Quick & Reilly   (800) 221-5220
Vanguard Discount Brokerage   (800) 992-8327
Waterhouse Securities   (800) 934-4410

Selected Mutual Funds

The simplest way to outperform most amateurs and professionals in most years—especially after tax considerations are included (see page 195)—is to buy an index fund with a very low expense ratio, like one of the Vanguard funds described below. Better still, make that *two* index funds: one that invests in U.S. stocks and one that invests abroad.

When you think about it, isn't this remarkable? With a single toll-free call, and a steady habit of periodic investing, you can set yourself up to outperform most professional money managers, and most of the people you know, for the rest of your life.

Who says investing has to be complex or time-consuming?

That said, here are a few more ideas. Please note that I have absolutely no connection to any of these firms. These are completely arm's-length recommendations. Note also that in not discussing the literally thousands of other funds available to you, I am doubtless omitting some that will do spectacularly well (if only I knew which!). But deluging you with alternatives is counterproductive. What you need is a handful of good alternatives and then, simply, to *get going*.

Here are four fund families with clear philosophies that will outlast any specific managers, with solid reputations for integrity, and with low expenses. They should be good choices for the next several decades. They allow easy switching between their various funds (but not between fund families themselves—for that you might want to utilize the services of a discount broker rather than dealing with the fund families directly—see pages 159–60).

Vanguard (800-662-7447). John Bogle founded this group in 1974 with the clear intention of making it the low-cost provider in the mutual fund field. He succeeded brilliantly. The average expense ratio of the Vanguard funds is less than half that of the second-place finisher. This is where you should go for index funds, as long as you can satisfy the minimum investment required (currently $3,000 in most cases). The Vanguard Total Stock Market Index Fund owns practically the entire U.S. stock market. The Vanguard Total International Index Fund does the same for the rest of the planet. In addition to their many domestic and international index funds, they have low-expense actively managed funds as well.

Tweedy, Browne (800-432-4789). This organization started as an investment advisory partnership in 1920 and counted the Dean of Investing himself, Benjamin Graham, as one of its clients. The partners learned from Graham the principles of value investing, and practiced it for their private clients for decades, before forming a couple of mutual funds in 1993—Tweedy, Browne American Value Fund and Tweedy, Browne Global Value Fund—to bring their expertise to the general public. They buy stocks the old-fashioned way: they hunt for the best bargains around. Both of their funds possess two characteristics that rarely go together: above-average performance and below-average volatility. Grafting the results of these funds onto the returns earned on their managed private accounts before that point shows an impressive average return of 20% over the past quarter century, while their "beta" (see Chapter 9) is only around 0.5. One nice touch is that the personal wealth of the partners is virtually all invested along with their clients. Minimum investment: $2,500.

Twentieth Century (800-345-2021). No two fund families could be more different than this and the previous one, but the funds of this group (now considered the aggressive side of the American Century fund family) have earned extraordinary results for 25 years as well. Formed in 1958 by James Stowers Jr. and now led by James Stowers III, all of the Twentieth Century funds formed prior to 1993 follow a strategy of looking for earnings and price momentum, and they succeed by riding winners as long as possible. Because the Stowers strategy is virtually a polar opposite to the Tweedy, Browne approach, this fund family's best years are often the worst years of Tweedy, Browne funds, and vice versa. Since growth stocks usually pay little or no dividends, and successful companies are generally held as long as they keep growing, the funds generate relatively little taxable income. You could achieve a rather neat balance by holding a Tweedy, Browne fund in a retirement account and a Twentieth Century fund in a taxable account. A warning: since the younger Stowers took over, he has added several funds with approaches his father never followed, and he also doesn't seem to share his father's fondness for small investors (historically, the funds had no minimum investment requirements), so new funds have been added to the group and minimum investments raised steadily in recent years (the most unfortunate being a $10,000 minimum for their emerging markets fund, the type of investment for which gradual and steady investment is most needed). Nevertheless, the younger Stowers, only around 40, has managed the older funds as competently as the old man ever did, and the team concept applied to these funds ensures that the philosophy will not change at least until the next generation of Stowerses takes over. Stick with the funds that pay virtually no dividends (so far, most of these still allow dollar-cost averaging starting as low as $50 per month) and you could enjoy a profitable ride. A dollar invested in Twentieth Century Growth fund in 1958 was worth $200 in early 1998. Just don't check your investment values during bear markets, or you'll develop a very painful ulcer. And if the stock market is high when you read this (it's certainly high as I write it), start with only a very modest investment and plan to dollar-cost-average for many years.

T. Rowe Price (800-638-5660). If you're a nervous newcomer and have only a little money, this fund family is waiting to adopt you. Formed in 1939 by T. Rowe himself, virtually all of their funds, including their money market funds, currently allow an investor to start with as little as $50 per month. (They even have one fund, T. Rowe Price Spectrum Growth Fund, that invests in several *other* Price funds, and would be a good first fund for anyone getting started with investing.) Their customer service reps are exceedingly patient, and they were either the first or among the first to pioneer such conveniences as Saturday and Sunday customer service, automatic monthly transfers from checking accounts to mutual funds (and vice versa), direct deposit of all or part of payroll and Social Security checks into investment accounts, and more. They have planning guides and informative brochures to help with many of the decisions discussed in this book, such as retirement and college planning and asset allocation. Their shareholder reports and newsletters are regularly rated the best in the business by mutual fund evaluation services. Yet with all this they have among the lowest expense ratios in the industry, and—like Vanguard, Twentieth Century, and Tweedy, Browne—all their funds are entirely without sales charges. Their funds are competently managed and diverse in scope. Frankly, anyone thinking of going to a financial planner might do better to call the T. Rowe Price group and just say: "I have no idea how to invest my money: can you help me?" You'll have to read and fill out the planners they send, but the results should be good and definitely won't turn out very bad, as they could with the wrong financial planner.

Fun with Compound Interest

If you have not yet learned how to work the compound interest key on your pocket calculator, or boot up a computer, but wish to astound your friends anyway, here is how $1 (or any multiple of $1) would grow at varying rates of interest, compounded annually. Unfortunately, if you are able to earn a very high rate of interest over a long period of time, it is likely to be because inflation is running at nearly as high a rate. Net of inflation and taxes, it's no cinch to earn 3% to 4% consistently, let alone any more. Still, it's fun to think about.

How a Dollar Grows*

Year	3%	5%	6%	7%	8%	10%	12%	15%	20%
1	$1.03	$1.05	$1.06	$1.07	$1.08	$1.10	$1.12	$1.15	$1.20
2	1.06	1.10	1.12	1.14	1.17	1.21	1.25	1.32	1.44
3	1.09	1.16	1.19	1.23	1.26	1.33	1.40	1.52	1.73
4	1.13	1.22	1.26	1.31	1.36	1.46	1.57	1.75	2.07
5	1.16	1.28	1.34	1.40	1.47	1.61	1.76	2.01	2.49
6	1.19	1.34	1.42	1.50	1.59	1.77	1.97	2.31	2.99
7	1.23	1.41	1.50	1.61	1.71	1.95	2.21	2.66	3.58
8	1.27	1.48	1.59	1.72	1.85	2.14	2.48	3.06	4.30
9	1.30	1.55	1.69	1.84	2.00	2.36	2.77	3.52	5.16
10	1.34	1.63	1.79	1.97	2.16	2.59	3.11	4.05	6.19
11	1.38	1.71	1.90	2.10	2.33	2.85	3.48	4.65	7.43
12	1.43	1.80	2.01	2.25	2.52	3.14	3.90	5.35	8.91
13	1.47	1.89	2.13	2.41	2.72	3.45	4.36	6.15	10.70
14	1.51	1.98	2.26	2.58	2.94	3.80	4.88	7.08	12.84
15	1.56	2.08	2.40	2.76	3.17	4.18	5.47	8.14	15.41
20	1.80	2.65	3.21	3.87	4.66	6.72	9.65	16.37	38.34
25	2.09	3.39	4.29	5.43	6.85	10.83	17.00	32.92	95.40
30	2.43	4.32	5.74	7.61	10.06	17.45	29.96	66.21	$237
35	2.81	5.52	7.69	10.68	14.79	28.10	52.80	$133	$591
40	3.26	7.04	10.29	14.98	21.72	45.26	93.05	$267	$1,469
50	4.38	11.47	18.42	29.47	46.90	$117	$289	$1,083	$9,100
100	$19	$132	$339	$868	$2,200	$13,780	$83,523	$1.17 million	$82.8 million
200	$369	$17,292	$115,125	$753,849	$4.8 million	$190 million	$7.0 billion	$1.4 trillion	$6.9 quadrillion

* To see how $3 or $1,000 or any other figure would grow, simply multiply by 3, or 1,000, or that other figure.

Still Not Sure
What to Do?

I do get a bit wordy. If everything you've read so far leaves you unsure what to do—frankly, I hope it hasn't—let me grab you by the hand and make it this simple:

Short of inheriting or marrying wealth, the surest way to become rich is to save at least 10% of all you earn and invest it for long-term growth. If you save at least 10% of each paycheck and earn a 7% annual return, it will take approximately 30 years to grow your nest egg to equal 10 years of income. You can then quit work and stay at approximately the same standard of living (earning enough to replace 70% of your previous income, but no longer needing to save 10%, pay Social Security tax on your earnings, or incur various job-related expenses). Or you can keep working and become *filthy* rich.

• **How do I save 10% of income?** If you have a retirement plan at work, just have 10% of your pay automatically saved. If not, set up an automatic monthly transfer from your checking account to your investment account. There is someone in the world making 10% less than you do who is not ragged and homeless. Try it.

• **How do I earn 7% per year?** That's the hard part, because the 7% has to be the *real* return, after taxes and inflation. In the bank, you will be lucky to stay even with inflation. But 7% isn't a pipe dream—over long periods, it's been the average real return for common stocks. You would have made around 7% per year for 30 years even if you had started investing at the beginning of 1929. Want just one idea? The T. Rowe Price Spectrum Growth Fund allocates shareholder money among nine different T. Rowe Price stock funds that invest in different parts of the U.S. and international markets, and allows investors to begin with as little as $50 per month. The effective annual expense ratio is well under 1% per year, making it one of the lowest cost funds available to small investors. Or choose a couple of even-lower-expense index funds instead. Either way, you'll do better than most of your friends and neighbors.

+ **Is that it?** Yes. If the stock market collapses, look at it as a great opportunity to make subsequent purchases at bargain prices. As much as possible, act as if the 10% you are investing has been spent, and don't touch any of it or its earnings until it reaches at least 10 times your annual salary. Then start spending up to 7% of it per year and it will never be exhausted. If you can, wait even longer to touch it, and spend even less than 7%.

+ **Can I get rich any faster?** No other investment category (even real estate) has produced long-term results exceeding those of common stocks. Aiming for higher returns is a good way to get lower returns. Saving more than 10% would definitely help, but for many families it's just too hard. The hardest part of making this system work is patience. Focus on your career, your family, your friends, and enjoying life to the fullest with the other 90% of your pay, so that the process of building wealth is as much fun as the result.

+ **What if I'm 63—is it too late to start?** Yes. But in my experience, the overwhelming majority of 63-year-olds who buy books about investing are those who've amassed a pretty good nest egg already. Good for you! Give this book to your kids.

Index

advertising, 34
age, 102
alcohol, 34
Allen, Woody, 147–48
American Express card, 18
annual reports, 156, 161–62
annuities, 105–7
antiques, 10
Apple Computer, 169
appliance insurance, 26
art, 10, 113–14
autographs, 10
automatic transfer investment
    plans, 48, 88, 228
autos
    financing, 19, 21–22, 23
    forced-place insurance, 29
    insurance, 20, 23–24
    Internet buying services, 26–27
    leasing, 21
    rental insurance, 26
    used, 20, 24
Avon, 124, 129, 138

B.F. Goodrich, 124
banks
    computer access, 45–46
    errors made by, 28–29
    savings accounts, 62–65, 86
Barron's, 144–45, 197
basis points, 54
Batra, Ravi, 199
bear markets, 122–23, 129–30,
    195
Beardstown Ladies, 52, 187n
Benchley, Robert, 41
Berkshire Hathaway Corporation,
    155

beta, 170, 223
Better Business Bureau, 114
*Blood in the Streets: Investment
    Profits in a World Gone Mad*
    (Davidson & Rees-Mogg),
    199
Bogle, John, 222
bond funds, 80–81
bonds
    vs. annuities, 106, 107
    callability, 70, 83, 85
    convertible, 82–83
    corporate, 79–80, 127
    inflation-adjusted, 77
    and interest rates, 70–71, 72
    junk, 80, 138
    municipal, 77–79, 85
    ratings, 69
    risk, 69–70
    Series EE savings, 86–88
    Treasury, 74, 76–77, 86, 179,
    199
    Treasury notes, 75–76
    unit trusts, 81–82
    war, 86
    zero-coupon, 83–85
brand names, 34
Braniff, 124
Broadway shows, 12
brokerage commissions and fees,
    55–56, 157–58
    annuities, 105
    bond funds, 81
    and broker/money manager
    performance, 151n
    and charity donations, 111
    and Internet investing, 185,
    186

random walk theory, 152–56, 173
real estate, 11, 29, 108–10. *See
also* mortgages
receipts, charity donations,
112–13
Rees-Mogg, William, 199
refinancing (mortgages), 20, 27
reimbursable expenses, 40
rent. *See* real estate
re-org, 183–84
Resorts International, 166
restaurants, 32–33
retirement plans, 93–105
and charity, 114–15
and children, 104–5
Keogh Plans, 96–99, 101–4,
106, 160
Roth IRAs, 99–101, 102,
103–4
SEPs, 96
vs. Education IRAs, 93
and zero-coupon bonds, 85
See also IRAs
return on equity, 123–24
Revlon Worldwide, 84
Revson, Charles, 15, 17
risk, 65–66, 67, 89
bond funds, 81
bonds, 69–70
mutual funds, 192
stocks, 76, 119–20, 127, 131,
145
zero-coupon bonds, 83–84
"Rocking-Horse Winner, The"
(Lawrence), 200–201
Rocky Mountain Institute, 30
Roth IRAs, 99–101, 102, 103–4
Rothchild, John, 187
Ruff, Howard, 199

Sahlins, Marshall, 201
"salary-reduction plans." *See*
401K plans; 403B plans
sales taxes, 14
Sam's Club, 17

Samson Properties 1985-A, *55–58*
Samuelson, Paul, 192
saving
and autos, 19, 20–24
and credit cards, 18, 21, 32–33
discount purchasing, 15–18, 35–
36, 205–6
energy, 29–30
frequent-flier miles, 18–19
and insurance, 24–26, 28–29
and Internet, 26–28
possibility of, 46–49
and tax brackets, 13–15
tax deductions, 30–31
See also budgeting; *specific
investments*
savings accounts, 62–65, 86
Savings Bank Life Insurance, 25
savings bonds, 86–88
SEC filings, 144
self-employment, 13, 96, 101, 110
selling short, 165–67, 168, 198n
SEPs (Simplified Employee
Pensions), 96
Series EE savings bonds, 86–88
Series HH "retirement" bonds, 87
Sheehy, Gail, 188–89
Sherrode, Blackie, 161
shorting (selling short), 165–67,
168, 198n
Sigel, Jeremy, 121
SIMPLEs (Savings Incentive
Match Plan for Employees),
96n
Simplified Employee Pensions. *See*
SEPs
smoking, 33–34
Social Security
benefits, 100–101, 211–14
and national debt, 215–17
tax, 13, 14
special offerings, 167–69
speculation, 145
Spiders, 198
splits, 163

spot secondaries. *See* special
  offerings
spreads, 169, 176, 186
stamps, 10, 11
Standard & Poor's, 69, 144
state income taxes, 13–14
  and corporate bonds, 79
  municipal bond exemption,
    77–78
  and Roth IRAs, 101
  savings bond exemption, 86
  and Treasury bills, 69
  and Treasury notes, 75
stock dividends, 164
Stock Guide (Standard & Poor's),
  144
stocks, 119–46
  annual reports, 156, 161–62
  vs. annuities, 106, 107
  bear markets, 122–23, 129–30
  beta, 170
  buy/sell timing, 131–35, 145
  charity donations, 111–12, 182
  charts, 162–63
  and convertible bonds, 82–83
  covered calls, 177–78
  daily quotations, 140
  vs. debt, 62
  diversification, 140
  dividend reinvestment plans,
    164–65
  Dow Jones Industrial Average,
    170–71, 172
  and 401K plans, 94–95
  and future predictions,
    199–200
  and hidden assets, 128–29
  high-fliers, 140–42
  holding, 137–40, 145
  hot tips, 135, 161
  index funds, 151–52, 185n,
    187n, 195, 198, 223
  and inflation, 11, 123, 128
  inside information, 135, 151,
    152, 162

and interest rates, 71–72
Internet trading, 185–86
investor information services,
  143–45
and junk bonds, 80
leverage, 171
limit orders, 167
margin, 71, 160, 171, 173
market irrationality, 125–26,
  131
"nifty fifty," 129–31
options, 157, 173–76
O-T-C (over-the-counter), 169
party quips, 219–20
penny, 179–80
periodic investment, 135–37
preferred, 85–86
price/earnings ratios, 127–28,
  140, 142–43
reasons for investing in, 119–24
relative value, 126–27
re-org, 183–84
risk, 76, 119–20, 127, 131, 145
vs. savings accounts, 62–63
selling short, 165–67, 168,
  198n
special offerings, 167–69
splits, 163
stock dividends, 164
and taxes, 110–11, 139–40,
  145–46, 181–82
VSP, 182–83
See also mutual funds
Stone Age Economics (Sahlins),
  201
store brands, 34
Stowers, James, III, 223
Stowers, James, Jr., 223
straddles, 176
strategic metals, 180

T. Rowe Price Group, 224–25,
  228–29
tax brackets, 90
  and homeownership, 110